Hebrew Learners' Dictionary

with Conjugation & Declension Tables,

Fully Transliterated – A1

Ahmet Murat TAŞER, PhD

2020

Hebrew Learners' Dictionary

with Conjugation & Declension Tables,

Fully Transliterated – A1

Ahmet Murat TAŞER, PhD

1. Edition / 2020

ISBN

9798695228137

COVER DESIGN & ILLUSTRATIONS by

Şeref Ali TAŞER

IMPRINT: INDEPENDENTLY PUBLISHED

THANKS TO

My family, standing by me at every step ...

BEFORE STARTING

This book was prepared with the intention to contribute to the resource material in Hebrew Language learning. For this reason, I hope this book would be a reference to all who need.

Ahmet Murat TAŞER, PhD

TABLE OF CONTENTS

INTRODUCTION

This **Quick-Reference-Mini 81-page Learners' Dictionary** contains **700** most common words and phrases. It is prepared for Hebrew learners at the beginner level. The words listed in this Learners' Dictionary are given only with the meaning for the learners at the beginning and intermediate levels. So, it should be noted that all meanings and variations may not be included.

This book includes the most common nouns, adjectives and verbs with the English transliteration.

The book also provides the declension tables of common propositions and conjugation tables of the most common verbs in the past, present and future tenses. Again, all the entries have an English transliteration.

Enjoy!

*****The dictionary section of this book is taken from the glossary section of the book "Comprehensive Hebrew for Beginners".*****

THE PRONUNCIATION KEY

WOWELS

a	as in "alphabet"	**o**	as in "toe"
e	as in "end"	**ɐ**	very short 'a'
u	as in "you"	**ə**	very short 'e'
ı	as in "color"	**θ**	very short 'o'
i	as in "in"		

CONSONANTS

b	as in "back"	**n**	as in "name"
c	as in "jump"	**p**	as in "pen"
ch	as in "chain"	**ph**	as in "fat"
d	as in "dumb"	**r**	as in "rock"
f	as in "fat"	**s**	as in "sweet"
g	as in "girl"	**sh**	as in "sheep"
h	as in "high"	**t**	as in "ten"
ħ	wheezy "h" sound	**v**	as in "vise"
k	as in "key"	**y**	as in "you"
l	as in "long"	**z**	as in "zero"
m	as in "man"		

<table>
<tr><td>

HEBREW-ENGLISH

</td><td>

עברית-אנגלית

</td></tr>
</table>

Since the Hebrew language is written from right to the left, this Learners' Dictionary is designed to read from right to left.

The words listed in this Learners' Dictionary are given only with the meaning for the learners at the beginning level. So, it should be noted that all meanings and variations may not be included.

Sometimes words can be found compound with some prefixes (ב, מ ,ה, ל); therefore, a word should be looked up after such prefixes are taken off of the stem of the word.

Verbs are listed by infinitive forms, meanings, and English transliteration.

The adjectives will be listed with the English transliteration respectively.

The nouns will be listed with the gender information with the transliteration to English respectively..

Since the similarity of the words Shin (שׁ) and Sin (שׂ), only Sin (שׂ) is dotted to simplify the usage by preventing the complexity of the dots.

father	*av (m)*		אב
dad	*aba (m)*		אבא
melon	*avatiaħ (m)*		אבטיח
spring	*aviv (m)*		אביב
but	*uval*		אבל
red	*adom*		אדום
Mr	*Adon*		אדון
or	*o*		או
August	*Ogust*		אוגוסט
ear	*ozen (f)*		אוזן
bus	*otobus (m)*		אוטובוס
food	*oħel (m)*		אוכל
perhaps	*ulai*		אולי
Departure Lounge	*olam-ha yotsi'im (m)*	*nos'im-ha*	אולם הנוסעים היוציאים
October	*Oktober*		אוקטובר
guest	*oreaħ,*		אורח
The same thing!	*Oto davar!*		אותו דבר!
brother	*aħ (m)*		אח

each other	*eħad le shnei*	אחד לשני
backward	*ahora*	אחורה
sister	*aħot (f)*	אחות
other	*aħer*	אחר
then	*aħar*	אחר
later	*aħar kaħ*	אחר כך
latest	*aharon (m)*	אחרון
then	*aħarei*	אחרי
It's not possible	*Eiy efshar + infinitivo*	אי אפשר
How nice!	*Eize yafe!*	איזה יפה!
slow	*iti*	איטי
What about you (f / m), you (pl)?	*Eiħ etsleħa (m), etslaħ (f), etslaħem?*	איך, אצלךֿ, אצלךֿ, אצלכם?
how?	*eiħ?*	איך?
Does not matter!	*Ein davar!*	אין דבר!
man, men (people)	*ish (m)*	איש
wife, woman	*isha (f)*	אישה
these	*Eile (m/f)*	אלה
if	*im*	אם
mother	*em (f)*	אם
mom	*ima (f)*	אמא
belief	*emuna (f)*	אמונה
American	*Amerikai*	אמריקאי
English (person / nationality)	*Angli*	אנגלי
England	*Anglia (f)*	אנגליה
English language	*Anglit (f)*	אנגלית
prohibited	*asur*	אסור
nose	*af (m)*	אף
none	*af eħad*	אף אחד
never	*af pa'am*	אף פעם
gray	*afor*	אפור
even	*afilu*	אפילו
April	*April*	אפריל
it's possible	*Efshar + infinitive*	אפשר
possible	*efshar*	אפשר

food	aruħa (f)	ארוחה
breakfast	aruħat boker (f)	ארוחת-בוקר
dinner	aruħat erev (f)	ארוחת-ערב
lunch	aruħat tsohoraim (f)	ארוחת-צהורייים
long	aruħ	ארוך
wallet	ernek (m)	ארנק
land, country	arets (f)	ארץ
the United States	Artsot Habrit (f)	ארצות-הברית
yesterday	etmol	אתמול
in	be	ב
really	be emet	באמת
please	bevakasha	בבקשה
You're welcome, please!	Bevakasha!	בבקשה!
clothes	beged (m)	בגד
swimwear	beged yam (m)	בגד-ים
absolutely, completely	bediyuk	בדיוק
usually	be dereħ klal	בדרך כלל
Come on (to a man).	Bo + to infinitive	בוא
Come on (to a woman).	Boi + to infinitive	בואי
Let's go!	Boi neleħ!	בואי נלך!
Certainly!	Be vadai!	בוודאי!
Good Morning! (in response)	Boker or!	בוקר אור!
Good Morning!	Boker tov!	בוקר טוב!
on sale	be zol	בזול
on time	be zman	בזמן
next month	be ħodesh ha ba	בחודש-הבא
last month	be ħodesh she avar	בחודש-שעבר
outside	be ħuts	בחוץ
youngester	baħur	בחור
smiling	beħiyuħ	בחיוך
exam	biħina (f)	בחינה
sure	batu'aħ	בטוח
Of course	betaħ	בטח
For sure!	Betaħ!	בטח!
stomach	beten (f)	בטן

together	be yaħad	ביחד
meanwhile	benta'im	בינתיים
egg	beitsa (f)	ביצה
home	bait (m)	בית
house	bait (m)	בית
hospital	beit ħolim (m)	בית-חולים
factory	beit ħaroshet (m)	בית-חרושת
high school	beit sefer tikon (m)	בית-ספר-טיכון
primary school	beit sefer yisudi (m)	בית-ספר-יסודי
coffee shop	beit kafe (m)	בית-קפה
without	bli	בלי
quickly	be mahirot	במהירות
especially	bimyuħad	במיוחד
all day	be mesheħ ha yom	במשך היום
all year	be mesheħ ha shana	במשך השנה
boy	ben (m)	בן
building	binyan (m)	בניין
Well!	Beseder!	בסדר!
in the end, finally	be sof	בסוף
in	be'od	בעוד
in a week	be'od shavu'a	בעוד שבוע
in an hour	be'od sha'a	בעוד שעה
in two hours	be'od sha'atayim	בעוד שעתיים
trouble	be'aya (f)	בעייה, בעיה
very nearly	be ereħ	בערך
soon	bekarov	בקרוב
first of all, at the beginning	breshit	בראשית
walking	baregel	ברגל
Welcome (m)!	Baruħ ha ba!	ברוך הבא!
Thank God!	Baruħ ha Shem!	ברוך השם!
clear	barur	ברור
healthy	bari'	בריא
pool	breħa	בריכה
next week	be shavu'a ha ba	בשבוע הבא
last week	be shavu'a she avar	בשבוע שעבר

for	*bishvil*	בשביל
nowhere	*be shum makom*	בשום מקום
next year	*be shana ha ba'a*	בשנה הבאה
last year	*be shana she avra*	בשנה שעברה
next hour	*be sha'a ha ba'a*	בשעה הבאה
last hour	*be sha'a she avra*	בשעה שעברה
meat	*basar (m)*	בשר
daughter	*bat (f)*	בת
girl	*bat (f)*	בת
Bon Appetite!	*Bete'avon!*	בתאבון!
inside	*betoħ*	בתוך
tall	*gavuha*	גָּבוּהַ
cheese	*gvina (f)*	גבינה
Ms.	*Gveret*	גברת
ceiling, roof	*gag (m)*	גג
big	*gadol*	גדול
body	*guf (m)*	גוף
guitar	*gitara (f)*	גיטרה
yard	*gina (f)*	גינה
too	*gam*	גם
a pair of socks	*garbaim (m/pl)*	גרביים
divorced	*garush*	גרוש
German (person / nationality)	*Germani (m)*	גרמני
Germany	*Germania (f)*	גרמניה
German language	*Germanit (f)*	גרמנית
rain	*geshem (m)*	גשם
thing	*davar (m)*	דבר
honey	*dvash (m)*	דבש
fish	*dag (m)*	דג
precisely	*davka*	דווקא
Similar to-	*dome le-*	דּוֹמֶה ל-
conversation, talk	*dibur (m)*	דיבור
host, butler	*dayal (m)*	דייל
apartment	*dira (f)*	דירה
December	*Detsember*	דצמבר

minute	daka (f)	דקה
south	darom	דרום
to the South	daroma	דרומה
passport	darkon (m)	דרכון
religion	dat (f)	דת
the most- (superlative form)	ha- be yoter	ה- ביותר
the land (Israel)	ha arets	הארץ
parents	horim (m/pl)	הורים
invitation	hazmana (f)	הזמנה
decision	haħlata (f)	החלטה
today	ha yom	היום
Here !, look!	Hine!	הינה!
The Wailing Wall (lit. The Western Wall)	Ha Kotel Ha Ma'aravi (m)	הכותל-המערבי
the most (superlative form)	haħi	הכי
Hello! (on the phone)	Halo!	הלו!
a lot	hamon	המון
Departures	hamar'ot	המראות
waiting, hesitation	hamtana (f)	המתנה
much, many	harbe	הרבה
and	ve	ו
rose	vered (m)	ורד
pink	varod	ורוד
this (f)	zot (f)	זאת
this (m)	ze (m)	זה
each other	ze et ze	זה את זה
one another	ze et ze	זה את זה
It's nice of you!	Ze yafe mitsedeyħem!	זה יפה מצדיכם!
each other	ze le ze	זה לזה
this (f)	zo (f)	זו
cheap	zol	זול
olives	zeitim (m/pl)	זיתים
hour	zman (m)	זמן
old age	zaken	זקן
scrambled eggs	ħavita (f)	חביתה

friend	*ħaver (m)*	חבר
room	*ħadar (m)*	חדר
dinning room	*ħadar ohel (m)*	חדראוכל
bath	*ħadar ambatya (m)*	חדר-אמבטייה
kids room	*ħadar yeladim (m)*	חדר-ילדים
living room	*ħadar megurim (m)*	חדר-מגורים
family room	*ħadar mishpaħa (m)*	חדר-משפחה
bedroom	*ħadar she'ina (m)*	חדר-שינה
new	*ħadash*	חדש
news	*ħadashot (f/pl)*	חדשות
month	*ħodesh (m)*	חודש
sick	*ħole*	חוֹלֶה
shirt	*ħultsa (f)*	חולצה
brown	*ħum*	חום
fever	*ħom (m)*	חום
high fever	*ħom gavoha (m)*	חום גבוה
coast	*ħof ha yam*	חוף-הים
holidays	*ħofsha (f)*	חופשה
winter	*ħoref (m)*	חורף
powerful	*ħazak*	חזק
smart	*ħaħam*	חכם
milk	*ħalav (m)*	חלב
window	*ħalon (m)*	חלון
weak	*ħalash*	חלש
hot	*ħam*	חם
It's hot outside!	*Ħam be ħuts!*	!חם בחוץ
I'm hot!	*Ħam li!*	!חם לי
butter	*ħem'a (f)*	חמאה
sour	*ħamuts*	חמוץ
store	*ħanut (f)*	חנות
parking place	*ħenion (m)*	חניון
God forbid!	*Ħas ve ħalila!*	!חס וחלילה
skirt	*ħatsait (f)*	חצאית
medium	*ħetsi (m)*	חצי
bitter, hot	*ħarif*	חריף

check	*ḥashbon (m)*	חשבון
important	*ḥashuv*	חשוב
electricity	*ḥashmal (m)*	חשמל
cat	*ḥatul (m)*	חתול
wedding	*ḥatuna (f)*	חתונה
bridegroom, boyfriend	*ḥatan (m)*	חתן
good	*tov*	טוב
Well!	*Tov!*	טוב!
Turkish (person / nationality)	*Turki*	טורקי
Turkey	*Turkiya (f)*	טורקיה
Turkish	*Turkit (f)*	טורקית
trip	*tiyul (m)*	טיול
flight	*tisa (f)*	טיסה
fool	*tipesh*	טיפש
telephone	*telfon (m)*	טלפון
delicious	*ta'im*	טעים
apple	*tapuaḥ ets (m)*	טפוח עץ
fresh	*tari*	טרי
hand	*yad (f)*	יד
July	*Yuli*	יולי
day	*yom (m)*	יום
birthday	*yom huledet (m)*	יום הולדת
Thursday	*yom ḥamishi (m)*	יום חמישי
Good day!	*Yom tov!*	יום טוב!
Sunday	*yom rishon (m)*	יום ראשון
Wednesday	*yom revi'i (m)*	יום רביעי
Saturday, Shabbat	*(yom) Shabat (f)*	יום שבת
Friday	*yom shlishi (m)*	יום שישי
Tuesday	*yom shlishi (m)*	יום שלישי
Monday	*yom shnei (m)*	יום שני
June	*Yuni*	יוני
Excellent! Wonderful!	*Yofi!*	יופי!
more than (comparative form)	*yoter me-*	יותר מ-
too much, too many	*yoter midai*	יותר מדי

can (ability, possibility)	*yaħol*	יכול
boy	*yeled (m)*	ילד
girl	*yalda (f)*	ילדה
children	*yeladim (m/pl)*	ילדים
sea	*yam (m)*	ים
right (not left)	*yamin*	ימין
on the right	*yamina*	ימינה
January	*Yanuar*	ינואר
nice	*yafe*	יָפֶה
exit	*yitsia (f)*	יציאה
expensive	*yakar*	יקר
green	*yarok*	ירוק
vegetable	*yerek (m)*	ירק
old	*yashan*	ישן
Israel	*Yisrael*	ישראל
Israeli	*Yisraeli (m)*	ישראלי
pain	*ke'ev (m)*	כאב
here	*kan*	כאן
when, while	*ka'asher*	כאשר
already	*kvar*	כבר
ball, tablet	*kadur (m)*	כדור
in order to	*kdei*	כדי
hat	*kova (m)*	כובע
power, strength	*ko'aħ (m)*	כוח
cup	*kos (f)*	כוס
cup made of glass	*kos-zħuħit (f)*	כוס-זכוכית
blue	*kaħol*	כחול
because	*ki*	כי
chair	*kise (m)*	כיסא
class	*kita (f)*	כיתה
all the time	*kol ha zman*	כל הזמן
all day	*kol ha yom*	כל היום
everyday	*kol yom*	כל יום
all kinds of	*kol mnei-*	-כל מני
every time, always	*kol pa'am*	כל פעם

dog	*kelev (m)*	כלב
bride	*kala (f)*	כלה
nothing at all	*klum*	כלום
very, a lot	*kol-kaħ*	כל-כך
a bunch of	*kol-kaħ harbe*	כל-כך הרבה
some, various	*kama*	כמה
How much?	*kama?*	כמה?
like, similar	*kmo*	כמו
almost	*kim'at*	כמעט
Yes!	*Ken!*	כן!
The Holy Sculpture (lit. The Church of the Tomb)	*Knesiyat Ha Kever (f)*	כניסת-הקבר
entry	*knisa (f)*	כניסה
money	*kesef (m)*	כסף
spoon	*kaf (m)*	כף
as usual	*ke ragil*	כרגיל
ticket	*kartis (m)*	כרטיס
sandwich	*kariħ (m)*	כריך
when, while	*kshe*	כש
address	*ktovet (f)*	כתובת
not but	*lo- ela-*	לא- אלא-
It's not comfortable for me!	*Lo nu'aħ li!*	לא נוח לי!
No!	*Lo!*	לא!
to love	*le'ehov*	לאהוב
to eat	*le'eħol*	לאכול
to say (used in present and past)	*lomar*	לאמור, לומר
where to?	*le'an?*	לאן?
single	*levad*	לבד
to check	*livdok*	לבדוק
to examine	*livdok*	לבדוק
come	*lavo'*	לבוא
white	*lavan*	לבן
to visit	*levaker*	לבקר
to ask for	*levakesh*	לבקש
to cook	*levashel*	לבשל

to talk to	*ledaber im*	לדבר עם
to know	*lada'at*	לדעת
to promise	*lehavti'aħ*	להבטיח
to bring	*lehavi*	להביא
to understand	*lehavin*	להבין
to get well	*lehavri*	להבריא
to say (used in present and future)	*lehagid*	להגיד
to arrive	*lehagi'a*	להגיע
to spend	*lehotsi*	להוציא
to order	*leħazmin*	להזמין
to invite to	*lehazmin le-*	להזמין ל-
to be	*lihiot*	להיות
to get in	*lehikanes*	להיכנס
to meet with	*lehipagesh (im)*	להיפגש עם
to stay	*lehisha'er*	להישאר
See you later!	*Lehitra'ot!*	להיתראות!
to prepare	*lehaħin*	להכין
to know, to be familiar with	*lehakir*	להכיר
to put in	*lehaħnis*	להכניס
to wait, to hesitate	*lehamtin*	להמתין
to reach an agreement	*lehaskim*	להסכים
to awaken	*leha'ir*	להעיר
to apologize	*lehitsta'er*	להצטער
to suggest	*lehatsi'a*	להציע
to have success in	*lehatsliaħ be-*	להצליח ב-
to feel	*lehargish*	להרגיש
to participate in	*lehishtatef be*	להשתתף
to be late	*lehitaħer*	להתאחר
to match with	*lehat'im le-*	להתאים ל-
to miss	*lehitga'age'a*	להתגעגע
to start	*lehatħil*	להתחיל
to get marry	*lehitħaten*	להתחתן
to wake up	*lehitorer*	להתעורר
to pray	*lehitpalel*	להתפלל

to get in contact with	lehitkasher le -/el -/im-	‏-להתקשר ל- /אל-/ עם
to get used to	lehitragel	להתרגל
to get excited	lehitragesh	להתרגש
to take a bath	lehitraḥets	להתרחץ
to come back from	laḥazor me- le-	‏-לחזור מ- ל
to wait	laḥakot	לחכות
to dream	laḥalom	לחלום
bread	leḥem (m)	לחם
to think	laḥashov	לחשוב
to fly	latus	לטוס
to wander, to take a walk	letayel	לטייל
Good night!	Laila tov!	‏!לילה טוב
to sleep	lishon	לישון
Have a good trip!	Leḥ le shalom!	‏!לך לשלום
to hurt	liḥ'ov	לכאוב
to write	lihtov	לכתוב
to get dressed	lilbosh	ללבוש
to study, to learn	lilmod	ללמוד
why?	lama?	‏?למה
to die	lamut	למות
to sell	limkor	למכור
to find	limtso	למצוא
for example	lemashal	למשל
to play (an instrument)	lenagen be-	‏-לנגן ב
to drive	linhog	לנהוג
to rest	lanu'aḥ	לנוח
to travel by	linso'a	‏-לנסוע ב
to clean	lenakot	לנקות
to fix, to arrange	lesader	לסדר
to finish	lesayem	לסיים
to work	la'avod	לעבוד
never (future tense)	le olam lo	לעולם לא
to leave	la'azov	לעזוב
to help	la'azor	לעזור
to cost	la'alot	לעלות

to answer	*la'anot al*	לענות על
to take a bath	*la'asot ambatya*	לעשות אמבטייה
to meet with	*lifgosh et*	לפגוש את
to be afraid of	*lifhod me-*	לפחוד מ-
prior to	*lifnei*	לפני
first of all	*lifnei ha kol*	לפני הכל
sometimes	*lif'amim*	לפעמים
to receive	*lekabel*	לקבל
to stand up	*lakum*	לקום
to drink	*lakahat*	לקחת
to buy	*liknot*	לקנות
to read	*likro'*	לקרוא
to see	*lir'ot*	לראות
to rain	*laredet*	לרדת
to cure	*lerape*	לרפא
to like	*lirtsot*	לרצות
to want	*lirtsot*	לרצות
to dance	*lirkod*	לרקוד
to annotate	*lirshom*	לרשום
to ask	*lish'ol*	לשאול
language	*lashon (f)*	לשון
to swim	*lishot*	לשחות
to sing	*lashir*	לשיר
to forget	*lishko'ah*	לשכוח
to rent	*liskor*	לשכור
to send	*lishlo'ah*	לשלוח
to pay	*leshalem*	לשלם
to hear	*lishmo'a*	לשמוע
to drink	*lishtot*	לשתות
from	*me-*	-מ
Hundred percent!	*Me'a ahuz!*	!מאה אחוז
much, many	*me'od*	מאוד
late	*mı'uhar*	מאוחר
disappointed	*me'uhzav*	מאוכזב
happy	*me'ushar*	מאושר

May	Mai	מאי
adult	mevugar	מבוגר
confused	mebulbal	מבולבל
too much, many	midai	מדי
country	medina (f)	מדינה
guide	medriħ (m)	מדריך
What happens?	Ma nishma?	?מה נשמע
For sure!	Ma she batu'aħ!	!מה שבטוח
How are you?	Ma shlomħa (m), shlomeħ (f), shlomħem (pl)?	?מה, שלומך, שלומך, שלומכם
quick	mahir	מהיר
engineer	mhandes	מהנדס
ready	muħan	מוכן
cab	monit (f)	מונית
helpful	mo'il	מועיל
early	mukdam	מוקדם
teacher	more	מורה
My sweet!	Motek!	!מותק
permitted	mutar	מותר
weather	mezeg-avir (m)	מזג-אויר
luggage, suitcase	mizvada (f)	מזוודה
briefcase	mizvadat-yad (f)	מזוודת-יד
secretary	mazkir	מזכיר
souvenir	mezkeret (f)	מזכרות
Congratulations!, good luck!	Mezel tov!	!מזל טוב
fork	mazleg (m)	מזלג
East	mizraħ	מזרח
to the East	mizraħa	מזרחה
notebook	maħberet (f)	מחברת
again	me ħadash	מחדש
price	meħir (m)	מחיר
disease	maħala (f)	מחלה
tomorrow	maħar	מחר
the day after tomorrow	moħrotayim	מחרתיים
computer	maħshev (m)	מחשב

idea	*maħsheva (f)*	מחשבה
thought	*maħsheva (f)*	מחשבה
kitchen	*mitbaħ (m)*	מטבח
plane	*matos (m)*	מטוס
umbrella	*mitriya (f)*	מטרייה
special	*meyuħad*	מיוחד
bed	*mita (f)*	מיטה
water	*ma'im (m/pl)*	מים
juice	*mits (m)*	מיץ
someone	*mishehu*	מישהו
car	*meħonit (f)*	מכונית
ugly	*meħo'ar*	מכוער
a pair of pants	*miħnasaim (m/pl)*	מכנסיים
letter	*miħtav (m)*	מכתב
salty	*malu'aħ*	מלוח
dirty	*meluħlaħ*	מלוכלך
hotel	*malon (m)*	מלון
salt	*melaħ (m)*	מלח
cucumber	*melafefeon (m)*	מלפפון
waiter	*meltsar*	מלצר
manager	*menahel*	מנהל
polite	*menumas*	מנומס
El Aksa Mosque	*Misgat-El Aktsa (m)*	מסגד-אל אקצה
match	*mesiba (f)*	מסיבה
restaurant	*mis'ada (f)*	מסעדה
enough	*maspik*	מספיק
phone number	*mispar-telfon (m)*	מספר-טלפון
wrong number	*mispar-taut (m)*	מספר-טעות
never (past tense)	*me olam lo*	מעולם לא
interesting	*meanyen*	מעניין
West	*ma'arav*	מערב
Westward	*ma'arava*	מערבה
key	*mafteaħ (f)*	מפתח
Wonderful!	*Metsuyan!*	מצוין!
site	*makom (m)*	מקום

profession, work	*miktso'a (m)*	מקצוע
fridge	*mkarer (m)*	מקרר
Mr	*Mar*	מר
March	*Mars/Merts*	מרס\מרץ
balcony	*mirpeset (f)*	מרפסת
soup	*marak (m)*	מרק
something	*mashehu*	משהו
boring	*mish'amem*	משעמם
family	*mishpaħa (f)*	משפחה
office	*misrad (m)*	משרד
sweet	*matok*	מתוק
when?	*matai?*	מתי?
gift	*matana (f)*	מתנה
driver	*nahag*	נהג
good nice	*nehedar*	נהדר
Well!	*Nu!*	נו!
November	*November*	נובמבר
relaxed	*nu'aħ*	נוח
It's okay with me this way!	*Nu'aħ li kaħa!*	נוח לי כך!
Okay for me!	*Nu'aħ li!*	נוח לי!
Let's see!	*Nir'e!*	ניראה!
Right!	*Naħon!*	נכון!
short, low	*namuħ*	נמוך
port	*namal (m)*	נמל
airport	*namal-te'ufa (m)*	נמל-תאופה
Have a good trip!	*Nesi'a tova!*	נסיע טובה!
nice	*naim*	נעים
Nice to meet you!	*Na'im me'od!*	נעים מאוד!
a pair of shoes	*na'alaim (m/pl)*	נעליים
clean	*naki*	נקי
excited	*nirgash*	נרגש
married	*nasuy*	נשוי
grandfather	*saba (m)*	סבא
neighborhood	*sviva (f)*	סביבה
grandmother	*savta (f)*	סבתא

closed	sagur	סגור
agency	soĥnot (f)	סוכנות
sugar	sukar (m)	סוכר
weekend	sof-ha shavu'a	סוף-השבוע
reason	siba (f)	סיבה
in total	saĥ ha kol	סך הכל
knife	sakin (m)	סכין
basket	sal (m)	סל
salad	salat (m)	סלט
Forgive me!	Sliĥa!	!סליחה
Shabbat meal	Saudat-Shabat (f)	סעודת-שבת
September	September	ספטמבר
book	sefer (m)	ספר
barber	sapar	סַפָּר
Spain	Sfarad (f)	ספרד
Spanish (person / nationality)	Sfaradi	ספרדי
Spanish language	Sfaradit (f)	ספרדית
movie	seret (m)	סרט
autumn	stav (m)	סתיו
work	avoda(f)	עבודה
for	avor	עבור
Hebrew	Ivrit (f)	עברית
tomato	agvaniya (f)	עגבנייה
until	ad	עד
still	adayin	עדיין
plus, more	od	עוד
not yet	od lo	עוד לא
in a minute soon	od me'at	עוד מעט
Anything else?	Od mashehu?	?עוד משהו
world	olam (m)	עולם
chicken	of (m)	עוף
tired	ayef	עייף
eye	ayin (m)	עין
city	iyr (f)	עיר
newspaper	iton (m)	עיתון

now	*aħshav*	עכשיו
about, on	*al*	על
with	*im*	עם
cloud	*anan (m)*	ענן
occupied	*asuk*	עסוק
nervous, furious	*atsbani*	עצבני
finger	*etsba (f)*	עצבע
sad	*atsuv*	עצוב
Good night!	*Erev tov!*	!ערב טוב
rich	*ashir*	עשיר
old	*atik*	עתיק
February	*Februar*	פברואר
meeting	*pgisha (f)*	פגישה
here	*po*	פה
mouth	*pe (m)*	פה
less than (comparative form)	*paħot me*	פחות מ
pepper	*pilpel (m)*	פלפל
unoccupied, free	*panui*	פנוי
one time	*pa'am*	פעם
slice	*prosa (f)*	פרוסה
flower	*peraħ (m)*	פרח
fruit	*priy (m)*	פרי
simply, in short	*pashut*	פשוט
open	*patu'aħ*	פתוח
colour	*tseva (m)*	צבע
yellow	*tsahov*	צהוב
plate	*tsalħat (f)*	צלחת
young	*tsa'ir*	צעיר
North	*tsafon*	צפון
to the North	*tsafona*	צפונה
crowded	*tsafuf*	צפוף
need, must	*tsariħ*	צריך
France	*Tsarfat (f)*	צרפת
French person	*Tsarfati*	צרפתי
French language	*Tsarfatit (f)*	צרפתית

group	kvutsa (f)	קבוצה
sacred	kadush	קדוש
ahead	kadima	קדימה
cashier	kupa'i	קופאי
little, small	katan	קטן
summer	ka'its (m)	קיץ
for summer	kaitsiim (m/pl)	קיציים
easy	kal	קל
Canada	Kanada (f)	קנדה
Canadian	Kanadai	קנדי
mall	kenion (m)	קניון
shopping	knia (f)	קנייה
coffee	kafe (m)	קפה
short	katsar	קצר
a little	katsat	קצת
cold	kar	קר
It's cold outside!	Kar be ḥuts!	!קר בחוץ
I'm cold!	Kar li!	!קר לי
near	karov	קרוב
cold	karir	קריר
difficult	kashe	קשה
head	rosh (m)	ראש
a lot, very	rov	רב
quarter (15 mins.)	reva (m)	רבע
leg	regel (f)	רגל
Just a second!	Rega!	!רגע
most of	rov ha-	-רוב ה
single	ravak	רווק
wind	ruaḥ (f)	רוח
Russian (person / nationality)	Rusi	רוסי
Russia	Rusiya (f)	רוסיה
Russian language	Rusit (f)	רוסית
doctor	rofe	רופאה
thin	raze	רזה
street	reḥov (m)	רחוב

far	rahok	רחוק
marmalade	riba (f)	ריבה
license	rishion (m)	רישיון
bad	ra	רע
hungry	ra'ev	רעב
noise	ra'ash (m)	רעש
only	rak	רק
that-	she-	‑ש
question	sh'ela (f)	שאלה
week	shavu'a (f)	שבוע
Good Shabbat!	Shabat Shalom!	!שבת שלום
airport	sde-te'ufa (f)	שדה‑תעופה
again	shuv	שוב
table	shulhan (m)	שולחן
dining table	shulhan ohel (m)	שולחן אוכל
nothing at all	shum davar	שום דבר
different from	shone me	שונֶה מ
market, shopping center	shuk (m)	שוק
black	shahor	שחור
dress	simla (f)	שימלה
song	shir (m)	שיר
bathroom, toilet	sheirutim (m/pl)	שירותים
neighbour	shahen	שכן
of (possessive)	shel	של
snow	sheleg (m)	שלג
Hi there!	Shalom!	!שלום
the day before yesterday	shlishom	שלשום
name	shem (m)	שם
there	sham, shama	שם, שמה
left	smol	שׂמאל
on the left	smola	שׂמאלה
happy	sameah	שמחַ
sky (heavens)	shmaim (m/pl)	שמיים
grease	shamen	שמן
year	shana (f)	שנה

Just a second!	*Shniya!*	‏שנייה!‏
hour	*sha'a (f)*	‏שעה‏
watch	*sha'on (m)*	‏שעון‏
wristwatch	*sha'on-yad (m)*	‏שעון־יד‏
gate	*sha'ar (m)*	‏שער‏
language	*safa (f)*	‏שפה‏
sack, bag	*sak (m)*	‏שק‏
Shekel (Israeli currency)	*Shekel (m)*	‏שקל‏
date	*ta'riħ (m)*	‏תאריך‏
Say hello to	*Tagid shalom le*	‏תגיד שלום ל־‏
tea	*te (f)*	‏תה‏
Thank you very much!	*Toda raba!*	‏תודה רבה!‏
Thank you!	*Toda!*	‏תודה!‏
line, queue	*tor (m)*	‏תור‏
handbag	*tik (m)*	‏תיק‏
shoulder bag	*tik-tsad (m)*	‏תיק־צד‏
Instantly!	*Teħef u miad!*	‏תכף ומיד!‏
Immediately!	*Teħef!*	‏תכף!‏
student	*talmid*	‏תלמיד‏
always	*tamid*	‏תמיד‏
menu	*tafrit (m)*	‏תפריט‏
medicine	*trufa (f)*	‏תרופה‏

ENGLISH - HEBREW
אנגלית עברית

English	Transliteration	Hebrew
a bunch of	*kol-kaħ harbe*	כל-כך הרבה
a little	*katsat*	קצת
a lot	*hamon*	המון
a lot, very	*rav*	רב
a pair of pants	*miħnasaim (m/pl)*	מכנסיים
a pair of shoes	*na'alaim (m/pl)*	נעליים
a pair of socks	*garbaim (m/pl)*	גרביים
about, on	*al*	על
absolutely, completely	*bediyuk*	בדיוק
adult	*mevugar*	מבוגר
address	*ktovet (f)*	כתובת
again	*me ħadash*	מחדש
again	*shuv*	שוב
agency	*soħnot (f)*	סוכנות
ahead	*kadima*	קדימה
airport	*namal-te'ufa (m)*	נמל-תאופה
airport	*sde-te'ufa (f)*	שדה-תעופה
all day	*be mesheħ ha yom*	במשך היום
all day	*kol ha yom*	כל היום
all kinds of	*kol mnei-*	כל מני-
all the time	*kol ha zman*	כל הזמן
all year	*be mesheħ ha shana*	במשך השנה
almost	*kim'at*	כמעט
already	*kvar*	כבר
always	*tamid*	תמיד
American	*Amerikai*	אמריקאי
and	*ve*	ו
Anything else?	*Od mashehu?*	עוד משהו?
apartment	*dira (f)*	דירה
apple	*tapuaħ ets (m)*	טפוח עץ
April	*April*	אפריל
as usual	*ke ragil*	כרגיל
August	*Ogust*	אוגוסט

autumn	stav (m)	סתיו
backward	aḥora	אחורה
bad	ra	רע
balcony	mirpeset (f)	מרפסת
ball, tablet	kadur (m)	כדור
barber	sapar	סַפָּר
basket	sal (m)	סל
bath	ḥadar ambatya (m)	חדר-אמבטייה
bathroom, toilet	sheirutim (m/pl)	שירותים
because	ki	כי
bed	mita (f)	מיטה
bedroom	ḥadar she'ina (m)	חדר-שינה
belief	emuna (f)	אמונה
big	gadol	גדול
birthday	yom huledet (m)	יום הולדת
bitter, hot	ḥarif	חריף
black	shaḥor	שחור
blue	kaḥol	כחול
body	guf (m)	גוף
Bon Appetite!	Bete'avon!	בתאבון!
book	sefer (m)	ספר
boring	mish'amem	משעמם
boy	ben (m)	בן
boy	yeled (m)	ילד
boyfriend, bridegroom	ḥatan (m)	חתן
bread	leḥem (m)	לחם
breakfast	aruḥat boker (f)	ארוחת-בוקר
bride	kala (f)	כלה
briefcase	mizvadat-yad (f)	מזוודת-יד
brother	aḥ (m)	אח
brown	ḥum	חום
building	binyan (m)	בניין
bus	otobus (m)	אוטובוס
but	aval	אבל
butter	ḥem'a (f)	חמאה

cab	monit (f)	מונית
can (ability, possibility)	yaħol	יכול
Canada	Kanada (f)	קנדה
Canadian	Kanadai	קנדי
car	meħonit (f)	מכונית
cashier	kupa'i	קופאי
cat	ħatul (m)	חתול
ceiling, roof	gag (m)	גג
Certainly!	Be vadai!	בוודאי!
chair	kise (m)	כיסא
cheap	zol	זול
check	ħashbon (m)	חשבון
cheese	gvina (f)	גבינה
chicken	of (m)	עוף
children	yeladim (m/pl)	ילדים
city	iyr (f)	עיר
class	kita (f)	כיתה
clean	naki	נקי
clear	barur	ברור
closed	sagur	סגור
clothes	beged (m)	בגד
cloud	anan (m)	ענן
coast	ħof ha yam	חוף-הים
coffee	kafe (m)	קפה
coffee shop	beit kafe (m)	בית-קפה
cold	kar	קר
cold	karir	קריר
colour	tseva (m)	צבע
come	lavo'	לבוא
Come on (to a man).	Bo + to infinitive	בוא
Come on (to a woman).	Boi + to infinitive	בואי
computer	maħshev (m)	מחשב
confused	mebulbal	מבולבל
Congratulations!, good luck!	Mezel tov!	מזל טוב!
conversation, talk	dibur (m)	דיבור

English	Transliteration	Hebrew
country	*medina (f)*	מדינה
crowded	*tsafuf*	צפוף
cucumber	*melafefeon (m)*	מלפפון
cup	*kos (f)*	כוס
cup made of glass	*kos-zhuhit (f)*	כוס-זכוכית
dad	*aba (m)*	אבא
date	*ta'rih (m)*	תאריך
daughter	*bat (f)*	בת
day	*yom (m)*	יום
December	*Detsember*	דצמבר
decision	*hahlata (f)*	החלטה
delicious	*ta'im*	טעים
Departure Lounge	*olam-ha nos'im-ha yotsi'im (m)*	אולם הנוסעים היוציאים
Departures	*hamar'ot*	המראות
different from	*shone me*	שונֶה מ
difficult	*kashe*	קשֶה
dining table	*shulhan ohel (m)*	שולחן אוכל
Dinner	*aruhat erev (f)*	ארוחת-ערב
dinning room	*hadar ohel (m)*	חדראוכל
dirty	*meluhlah*	מלוכלך
disappointed	*me'uhzav*	מאוכזב
disease	*mahala (f)*	מחלה
divorced	*garush*	גרוש
doctor	*rofe*	רופֵא
Does not matter!	*Ein davar!*	אין דבר!
dog	*kelev (m)*	כלב
dress	*simla (f)*	שימלה
driver	*nahag*	נהג
each other	*ehad le shnei*	אחד לשני
each other	*ze et ze*	זה את זה
each other	*ze le ze*	זה לזה
ear	*ozen (f)*	אוזן
early	*mukdam*	מוקדם
East	*mizrah*	מזרח
easy	*kal*	קל

egg	beitsa (f)	ביצה
El Aksa Mosque	Misgat-El Aktsa (m)	מסגד-אל אקצה
electricity	ħashmal (m)	חשמל
engineer	mhandes	מהנדס
England	Anglia (f)	אנגליה
English (person / nationality)	Angli	אנגלי
English language	Anglit (f)	אנגלית
enough	maspik	מספיק
entry	knisa (f)	כניסה
especially	bimyuħad	במיוחד
even	afilu	אפילו
every time, always	kol pa'am	כל פעם
everyday	kol yom	כל יום
exam	biħina (f)	בחינה
Excellent! Wonderful!	Yofi!	יופי!
excited	nirgash	נרגש
Exit	yitsia (f)	יציאה
expensive	yakar	יקר
eye	ayin (m)	עין
factory	beit ħaroshet (m)	בית-חרושת
family	mishpaħa (f)	משפחה
family room	ħadar mishpaħa (m)	חדר-משפחה
far	raħok	רחוק
father	av (m)	אב
February	Februar	פברואר
fever	ħom (m)	חום
finger	etsba (f)	עצבע
first of all	lifnei ha kol	לפני הכל
first of all, at the beginning	breshit	בראשית
fish	dag (m)	דג
flight	tisa (f)	טיסה
flower	peraħ (m)	פרח
food	oħel (m)	אוכל
food	aruħa (f)	ארוחה

fool	tipesh	טיפש
for	bishvil	בשביל
for	avor	עבור
for example	lemashal	למשל
for summer	kaitsiim (m/pl)	קיציים
For sure!	Betaħ!	בטח!
For sure!	Ma she batu'aħ!	מה שבטוח!
Forgive me!	Sliħa!	סליחה!
fork	mazleg (m)	מזלג
France	Tsarfat (f)	צרפת
French language	Tsarfatit (f)	צרפתית
French person	Tsarfati	צרפתי
fresh	tari	טרי
Friday	yom shlishi (m)	יום שישי
fridge	mkarer (m)	מקרר
friend	ħaver (m)	חבר
from	me-	‫מ-‬
fruit	priy (m)	פרי
gate	sha'ar (m)	שער
German (person / nationality)	Germani (m)	גרמני
German language	Germanit (f)	גרמנית
Germany	Germania (f)	גרמניה
gift	matana (f)	מתנה
girl	bat (f)	בת
girl	yalda (f)	ילדה
God forbid!	Ħas ve ħalila!	חס וחלילה!
good	tov	טוב
Good day!	Yom tov!	יום טוב!
Good Morning!	Boker tov!	בוקר טוב!
Good Morning! (in response)	Boker or!	בוקר אור!
good nice	nehedar	נהדר
Good night!	Erev tov!	ערב טוב!
Good Shabbat!	Shabat Shalom!	שבת שלום!
Goodnight!	Laila tov!	לילה טוב!

English	Transliteration	Hebrew
grandfather	saba (m)	סבא
grandmother	savta (f)	סבתא
gray	afor	אפור
grease	shamen	שמן
green	yarok	ירוק
group	kvutsa (f)	קבוצה
guest	oreaħ,	אורח
guide	medriħ (m)	מדריך
guitar	gitara (f)	גיטרה
hand	yad (f)	יד
handbag	tik (m)	תיק
happy	me'ushar	מאושר
happy	sameaħ	שמח
hat	kova (m)	כובע
Have a good trip!	Leħ le shalom!	לך לשלום!
Have a good trip!	Nesi'a tova!	נסיע טובה!
head	rosh (m)	ראש
healthy	bari'	בריא
Hebrew	Ivrit (f)	עברית
Hello! (on the phone)	Halo!	הלו!
helpful	mo'il	מועיל
here	kan	כאן
here	po	פה
Here !, look!	Hine!	הינה!
Hi there!	Shalom!	שלום!
high fever	ħom gavoha (m)	חום גבוה
high school	beit sefer tikon (m)	בית-ספר-טיכון
holidays	ħofsha (f)	חופשה
home	bait (m)	בית
honey	dvash (m)	דבש
hospital	beit ħolim (m)	בית חולים
host, butler	dayal (m)	דייל
hot	ħam	חם
hotel	malon (m)	מלון
hour	zman (m)	זמן

hour	sha'a (f)	שעה
house	bait (m)	בית
How are you?	Ma shlomħa (m), shlomeħ (f), shlomħem (pl)?	מה, שלומךָ, שלומךְ, שלומכם?
How much?	kama?	כמה?
How nice!.	Eize yafe!	איזה יפה!
how?	eiħ?	איך?
Hundred percent!	Me'a aħuz!	מאה אחוז!
hungry	ra'ev	רעב
idea	maħsheva (f)	מחשבה
if	im	אם
I'm cold!	Kar li!	קר לי!
I'm hot!	Ħam li!	חם לי!
Immediately!	Teħef!	תכף!
important	ħashuv	חשוב
in	be	ב
in	be'od	בעוד
in a minute soon	od me'at	עוד מעט
in a week	be'od shavu'a	בעוד שבוע
in an hour	be'od sha'a	בעוד שעה
in order to	kdei	כדי
in the end, finally	be sof	בסוף
in total	saħ ha kol	סך הכל
in two hours	be'od sha'atayim	בעוד שעתיים
inside	betoħ	בתוך
Instantly!	Teħef u miad!	תכף ומיד!
interesting	meanyen	מעניין
invitation	hazmana (f)	הזמנה
Israel	Yisrael	ישראל
Israeli	Yisraeli (m)	ישראלי
It's cold outside!	Kar be ħuts!	קר בחוץ!
It's hot outside!	Ħam be ħuts!	חם בחוץ!
It's nice of you!	Ze yafe mitsedeyħem!	זה יפה מצדיכם!
It's not comfortable for me!	Lo nu'aħ li!	לא נוח לי!
It's not possible	Eiy efshar + infinitivo	אי אפשר

It's okay with me this way!	*Nu'ah li kaha!*	נוח לי כך!
it's possible	*Efshar + infinitive*	אפשר
January	*Yanuar*	ינואר
juice	*mits (m)*	מיץ
July	*Yuli*	יולי
June	*Yuni*	יוני
Just a second!	*Rega!*	רגע!
Just a second!	*Shniya!*	שנייה!
key	*mafteah (f)*	מפתח
kids room	*hadar yeladim (m)*	חדר-ילדים
kitchen	*mitbah (m)*	מטבח
knife	*sakin (m)*	סכין
land, country	*arets (f)*	ארץ
language	*lashon (f)*	לשון
language	*safa (f)*	שׂפה
last hour	*be sha'a she avra*	בשעה שעברה
last month	*be hodesh she avar*	בחודש-שעבר
last week	*be shavu'a she avar*	בשבוע שעבר
last year	*be shana she avra*	בשנה שעברה
late	*mı'uhar*	מאוחר
later	*ahar kah*	אחר כך
latest	*aharon (m)*	אחרון
left	*smol*	שׂמאל
leg	*regel (f)*	רגל
less than (comparative)	*pahot me*	פחות מ
Let's go!	*Boi neleh!*	בואי נלך!
Let's see!	*Nir'e!*	נראה!
letter	*mihtav (m)*	מכתב
license	*rishion (m)*	רישיון
like, similar	*kmo*	כמו
line, queue	*tor (m)*	תור
little, small	*katan*	קטן
living room	*hadar megurim (m)*	חדר-מגורים
long	*aruh*	ארוך
luggage, suitcase	*mizvada (f)*	מזוודה

lunch	aruħat tsohoraim (f)	ארוחת-צהריים
mall	kenion (m)	קניון
man, men (people)	ish (m)	איש
manager	menahel	מנהל
March	Mars/Merts	מרס\מרץ
market, shopping center	shuk (m)	שוק
marmalade	riba (f)	ריבה
married	nasuy	נשוי
match	mesiba (f)	מסיבה
May	Mai	מאי
meanwhile	benta'im	בינתיים
meat	basar (m)	בשר
medicine	trufa (f)	תרופה
medium	ħetsi (m)	חצי
meeting	pgisha (f)	פגישה
melon	avatiaħ (m)	אבטיח
menu	tafrit (m)	תפריט
milk	ħalav (m)	חלב
minute	daka (f)	דקה
mom	ima (f)	אמא
Monday	yom shnei (m)	יום שני
money	kesef (m)	כסף
month	ħodesh (m)	חודש
more than (comparative)	yoter me-	יותר מ-
most of	rov ha-	רוב ה-
mother	em (f)	אם
mouth	pe (m)	פה
movie	seret (m)	סרט
Mr	Adon	אדון
Mr	Mar	מר
Ms.	Gveret	גברת
much, many	harbe	הרבה
much, many	me'od	מאוד
My sweet!	Motek!	מותק!
name	shem (m)	שם

near	*karov*	קרוב
need, must	*tsariħ*	צריך
neighborhood	*sviva (f)*	סביבה
neighbour	*shaħen*	שכן
nervous, furious	*atsbani*	עצבני
never	*af pa'am*	אף פעם
never (future tense)	*le olam lo*	לעולם לא
never (past tense)	*me olam lo*	מעולם לא
new	*ħadash*	חדש
news	*ħadashot (f/pl)*	חדשות
newspaper	*iton (m)*	עיתון
next hour	*be sha'a ha ba'a*	בשעה הבאה
next month	*be ħodesh ha ba*	בחודש-הבא
next week	*be shavu'a ha ba*	בשבוע הבא
next year	*be shana ha ba'a*	בשנה הבאה
nice	*yafe*	יָפֶה
nice	*naim*	נעים
Nice to meet you!	*Na'im me'od!*	נעים מאוד!
No!	*Lo!*	לא!
noise	*ra'ash (m)*	רעש
none	*af eħad*	אף אחד
North	*tsafon*	צפון
nose	*af (m)*	אף
not but	*lo- ela-*	לא- אלא-
not yet	*od lo*	עוד לא
notebook	*maħberet (f)*	מחברת
nothing at all	*klum*	כלום
nothing at all	*shum davar*	שום דבר
November	*November*	נובמבר
now	*aħshav*	עכשיו
nowhere	*be shum makom*	בשום מקום
occupied	*asuk*	עסוק
October	*Oktober*	אוקטובר
of (possessive)	*shel*	של
Of course	*betaħ*	בטח

office	*misrad (m)*	משרד
Okay for me!	*Nu'aḥ li!*	!נוח לי
old	*yashan*	ישן
old	*atik*	עתיק
old age	*zaken*	זקן
olives	*zeitim (m/pl)*	זיתים
on sale	*be zol*	בזול
on the left	*smola*	שמאלה
on the right	*yamina*	ימינה
on time	*be zman*	בזמן
one another	*ze et ze*	זה את זה
one time	*pa'am*	פעם
only	*rak*	רק
open	*patu'aḥ*	פתוח
or	*o*	או
other	*aḥer*	אחר
outside	*be ḥuts*	בחוץ
pain	*ke'ev (m)*	כאב
parents	*horim (m/pl)*	הורים
parking place	*ḥenion (m)*	חניון
passport	*darkon (m)*	דרכון
pepper	*pilpel (m)*	פלפל
perhaps	*ulai*	אולי
permitted	*mutar*	מותר
phone number	*mispar-telfon (m)*	מספר-טלפון
pink	*varod*	ורוד
plane	*matos (m)*	מטוס
plate	*tsalḥat (f)*	צלחת
please	*bevakasha*	בבקשה
plus, more	*od*	עוד
polite	*menumas*	מנומס
pool	*breḥa*	בריכה
port	*namal (m)*	נמל
possible	*efshar*	אפשר
power, strength	*ko'aḥ (m)*	כוח

powerful	ḥazak	חזק
precisely	davka	דווקא
price	meḥir (m)	מחיר
primary school	beit sefer yisudi (m)	בית-ספר-יסודי
prior to	lifnei	לפני
profession, work	miktso'a (m)	מקצוע
prohibited	asur	אסור
question	sh'ela (f)	שאלה
quarter (15 mins.)	reva (m)	רבע
quick	mahir	מהיר
quickly	be mahirot	במהירות
rain	geshem (m)	גשם
ready	muḥan	מוכן
Really	be emet	באמת
reason	siba (f)	סיבה
Red	adom	אדום
relaxed	nu'aḥ	נוח
religion	dat (f)	דת
restaurant	mis'ada (f)	מסעדה
rich	ashir	עשיר
right (not left)	yamin	ימין
Right!	Naḥon!	נכון!
room	ḥadar (m)	חדר
rose	vered (m)	ורד
Russia	Rusiya (f)	רוסיה
Russian (person / nationality)	Rusi	רוסי
Russian language	Rusit (f)	רוסית
sack, bag	sak (m)	שק
sacred	kadush	קדוש
sad	atsuv	עצוב
salad	salat (m)	סלט
salt	melaḥ (m)	מלח
salty	malu'aḥ	מלוח
sandwich	kariḥ (m)	כריך
Saturday, Shabbat	(yom) Shabat (f)	יום שבת

Say hello to	*Tagid shalom le*	-תגיד שלום ל
scrambled eggs	*ħavita (f)*	חביתה
sea	*yam (m)*	ים
secretary	*mazkir*	מזכיר
See you later!	*Lehitra'ot!*	!להיתראות
September	*September*	ספטמבר
Shabbat meal	*Saudat-Shabat (f)*	סעודת-שבת
Shekel (Israeli currency)	*Shekel (m)*	שקל
shirt	*ħultsa (f)*	חולצה
shopping	*knia (f)*	קנייה
short	*katsar*	קצר
short, low	*namuħ*	נמוך
shoulder bag	*tik-tsad (m)*	תיק-צד
sick	*ħole*	חולֶה
Similar to-	*dome le-*	-דומֶה ל
simply, in short	*pashut*	פשוט
single	*levad*	לבד
single	*ravak*	רווק
sister	*aħot (f)*	אחות
site	*makom (m)*	מקום
skirt	*ħatsait (f)*	חצאית
sky (heavens)	*shmaim (m/pl)*	שמיים
slice	*prosa (f)*	פרוסה
slow	*iti*	איטי
smart	*ħaħam*	חכם
smiling	*beħiyuħ*	בחיוך
snow	*sheleg (m)*	שלג
some, various	*kama*	כמה
someone	*mishehu*	מישהו
something	*mashehu*	משהו
sometimes	*lif'amim*	לפעמים
son	*ben (m)*	בן
song	*shir (m)*	שיר
soon	*bekarov*	בקרוב
soup	*marak (m)*	מרק

sour	ħamuts	חמוץ
south	darom	דרום
souvenir	mezkeret (f)	מזכרות
Spain	Sfarad (f)	ספרד
Spanish (person / nationality)	Sfaradi	ספרדי
Spanish language	Sfaradit (f)	ספרדית
special	meyuħad	מיוחד
spoon	kaf (m)	כף
spring	aviv (m)	אביב
still	adayin	עדיין
stomach	beten (f)	בטן
store	ħanut (f)	חנות
street	reħov (m)	רחוב
student	talmid	תלמיד
sugar	sukar (m)	סוכר
summer	ka'its (m)	קיץ
Sunday	yom rishon (m)	יום ראשון
sure	batu'aħ	בטוח
sweet	matok	מתוק
swimwear	beged yam (m)	בגד-ים
table	shulħan (m)	שולחן
tall	gavuha	גָבוהַ
tea	te (f)	תה
teacher	more	מוֹרֶה
telephone	telfon (m)	טלפון
Thank God!	Baruħ ha Shem!	ברוך השם!
Thank you very much!	Toda raba!	תודה רבה!
Thank you!	Toda!	תודה!
that-	she-	ש-
the day after tomorrow	moħrotayim	מחרתיים
the day before yesterday	shlishom	שלשום
The Holy Sculpture	Knesiyat Ha Kever (f)	כניסת-הקבר
the land (Israel)	ha arets	הארץ
the most (superlative)	haħi	הכי
the most- (superlative)	ha- be yoter	ה- ביותר

The same thing!	Oto davar!	אותו דבר!
the United States	Artsot Habrit (f)	ארצות-הברית
The Wailing Wall	Ha Kotel Ha Ma'aravi (m)	הכותל-המערבי
then	aḥar	אחר
then	aḥarei	אחרי
there	sham, shama	שם, שמה
these	Eile (m/f)	אלה
thin	raze	רָזֶה
thing	davar (m)	דבר
this (f)	zot (f)	זאת
this (f)	zo (f)	זו
this (m)	ze (m)	זה
thought	maḥsheva (f)	מחשבה
Thursday	yom ḥamishi (m)	יום חמישי
ticket	kartis (m)	כרטיס
tired	ayef	עייף
to annotate	lirshom	לרשום
to answer	la'anot al	לענות על
to apologize	lehitsta'er	להצטער
to arrive	lehagi'a	להגיע
to ask	lish'ol	לשאול
to ask for	levakesh	לבקש
to wake up	lehitorer	להתעורר
to be	lihiot	להיות
to be afraid of	lifḥod me-	לפחוד מ-
to be late	lehitaḥer	להתאחר
to bring	lehavi	להביא
to buy	liknot	לקנות
to check	livdok	לבדוק
to clean	lenakot	לנקות
to cook	levashel	לבשל
to cost	la'alot	לעלות
to cure	lerape	לרפא
to dance	lirkod	לרקוד
to die	lamut	למות

to dream	*laḥalom*	לחלום
to drink	*lakaḥat*	לקחת
to drink	*lishtot*	לשתות
to drive	*linhog*	לנהוג
to eat	*le'eḥol*	לאכול
to examine	*livdok*	לבדוק
to feel	*lehargish*	להרגיש
to find	*limtso*	למצוא
to finish	*lesayem*	לסיים
to fix, to arrange	*lesader*	לסדר
to fly	*latus*	לטוס
to forget	*lishko'aḥ*	לשכוח
to get dressed	*lilbosh*	ללבוש
to get excited	*lehitragesh*	להתרגש
to get in	*lehikanes*	להיכנס
to get in contact with	*lehitkasher le -/el -/im-*	להתקשר ל- /אל-/ עם-
to get marry	*lehitḥaten*	להתחתן
to get used to	*lehitragel*	להתרגל
to get well	*lehavri*	להבריא
to have success in	*lehatsliaḥ be-*	להצליח ב-
to hear	*lishmo'a*	לשמוע
to help	*la'azor*	לעזור
to hurt	*liḥ'ov*	לכאוב
to invite to	*lehazmin le-*	להזמין ל-
to know	*lada'at*	לדעת
to know, to be familiar with	*lehakir*	להכיר
to leave	*la'azov*	לעזוב
to like	*lirtsot*	לרצות
to love	*le'ehov*	לאהוב
to match with	*lehat'im le-*	להתאים ל-
to meet with	*lehipagesh (im)*	להיפגש עם
to meet with	*lifgosh et*	לפגוש את
to miss	*lehitga'age'a*	להתגעגע
to order	*lehazmin*	להזמין
to participate in	*lehishtatef be*	להשתתף

to pay	*leshalem*	לשלם
to play (an instrument)	*lenagen be-*	לנגן ב-
to pray	*lehitpalel*	להתפלל
to prepare	*lehaḥin*	להכין
to promise	*lehavti'aḥ*	להבטיח
to put in	*lehaḥnis*	להכניס
to rain	*laredet*	לרדת
to reach an agreement	*lehaskim*	להסכים
to read	*likro'*	לקרוא
to receive	*lekabel*	לקבל
to rent	*liskor*	לשׂכור
to rest	*lanu'aḥ*	לנוח
to say (present and future)	*lehagid*	להגיד
to say (present and past)	*lomar*	לאמור, לומר
to see	*lir'ot*	לראות
to sell	*limkor*	למכור
to send	*lishlo'aḥ*	לשלוח
to sing	*lashir*	לשיר
to sit down	*lashevet*	לשבת
to sleep	*lishon*	לישון
to spend	*lehotsi*	להוציא
to stand up	*lakum*	לקום
to start	*lehatḥil*	להתחיל
to stay	*lehisha'er*	להישאר
to study, to learn	*lilmod*	ללמוד
to suggest	*lehatsi'a*	להציע
to swim	*lisḥot*	לשׂחות
to take a bath	*lehitraḥets*	להתרחץ
to take a bath	*la'asot ambatya*	לעשות אמבטייה
to talk to	*ledaber im*	לדבר עם
to the East	*mizraḥa*	מזרחה
to the North	*tsafona*	צפונה
to the South	*daroma*	דרומה
to think	*laḥashov*	לחשוב
to travel by	*linso'a*	לנסוע ב-

to understand	lehavin	להבין
to visit	levaker	לבקר
to wait	laħakot	לחכות
to wait, to hesitate	lehamtin	להמתין
to awaken	leha'ir	להעיר
to wander, to take a walk	letayel	לטייל
to want	lirtsot	לרצות
to work	la'avod	לעבוד
to write	liħtov	לכתוב
to-come back from	laħazor me- le-	לחזור מ- ל-
today	ha yom	היום
together	be yaħad	ביחד
tomato	agvaniya (f)	עגבנייה
tomorrow	maħar	מחר
too	gam	גם
too much, many	yoter midai	יותר מדי
too much, many	midai	מדי
trip	tiyul (m)	טיול
trouble	be'aya (f)	בעייה, בעיה
Tuesday	yom shlishi (m)	יום שלישי
Turkey	Turkiya (f)	טורקיה
Turkish	Turkit (f)	טורקית
Turkish (person / nationality)	Turki	טורקי
ugly	meħo'ar	מכוער
umbrella	mitriya (f)	מטרייה
unoccupied, free	panui	פנוי
until	ad	עד
usually	be dereħ klal	בדרך כלל
vegetable	yerek (m)	ירק
very nearly	be ereħ	בערך
very, a lot	kol-kaħ	כל-כך
waiter	meltsar	מלצר
waiting, hesitation	hamtana (f)	המתנה
walking	baregel	ברגל
wallet	ernek (m)	ארנק

watch	sha'on (m)	שעון
water	ma'im (m/pl)	מים
weak	ħalash	חלש
weather	mezeg-avir (m)	מזג-אוויר
wedding	ħatuna (f)	חתונה
Wednesday	yom revi'i (m)	יום רביעי
week	shavu'a (f)	שבוע
weekend	sof-ha shavu'a	סוף-השבוע
Welcome (m)!	Baruħ ha ba!	ברוך הבא!
Well!	Beseder!	בסדר!
Well!	Tov!	טוב!
Well!	Nu!	נו!
West	ma'arav	מערב
Westward	ma'arava	מערבה
What about you (f / m), (pl)?	Eiħ etsleħa (m), etslaħ (f), etslaħem?	איך, אצלך, אצלך, אצלכם?
What happens?	Ma nishma?	מה נשמע?
when, while	ka'asher	כאשר
when, while	kshe	כש
when?	matai?	מתי?
where to?	le'an?	לאן?
white	lavan	לבן
why?	lama?	למה?
wife, woman	isha (f)	אישה
wind	ruaħ (f)	רוח
window	ħalon (m)	חלון
winter	ħoref (m)	חורף
with	im	עם
without	bli	בלי
Wonderful!	Metsuyan!	מצוין!
work	avoda(f)	עבודה
world	olam (m)	עולם
wristwatch	sha'on-yad (m)	שעון-יד
wrong number	mispar-taut (m)	מספר-טעות
yard	gina (f)	גינה

year	*shana (f)*	שנה
yellow	*tsahov*	צהוב
Yes!	*Ken!*	כן!
Yesterday	*etmol*	אתמול
You're welcome, please!	*Bevakasha!*	בבקשה!
young	*tsa'ir*	צעיר
youngester	*baħur*	בחור

ADDITIONAL_GRAMMAR: 1   דקדוק_נוסף

DECLENSION OF SOME COMMON PREPOSITIONS

In this part, declension tables of some common prepositions are listed.

Declension of the Common Prepositions "at one's place"(אצל), "with" (עם), and "to, towards" (אל)

אל		עם		אצל		Subject Pronoun
אלי	elai	איתי	iti	אצלי	etsli	אני
אליך	elaħa	איתך	itħa	אצלך	etsleħa	אתה
אליך	elaiħ	איתך	itaħ	אצלך	etslaħ	את
אליו	elav	איתו	ito	אצלו	etslo	הוא
אליה	eleha	איתה	ita	אצלה	etsla	היא
אלינו	elanu	איתנו	itanu	אצלנו	etslanu	אנחנו
אליכם	eleħem	איתכם	itħem	אצלכם	etslaħem	אתם
אליכן	eleħen	איתכן	itħen	אצלכן	etslaħen	אתן
אליהם	elehem	איתם	itam	אצלם	etslam	הם
אליהן	elehen	איתן	itan	אצלן	etslan	הן

Declension of the Common Prepositions "on top of & about"(עַל), "for" (בשביל), and "from" (מ)

מ		בשביל		עַל		Subject Pronoun
ממני	mimeni	בשבילי	bishvili	עלי	alai	אני
ממך	mimħa	בשבילך	bishvilħa	עליך	aleħa	אתה
ממך	mimeħ	בשבילך	bishvileħ	עליך	alaiħ	את
ממנו	mimenu	בשבילו	bishvilo	עליו	alav	הוא
ממנה	mimena	בשבילה	bishvila	עליך	aleha	היא
מאיתנו\ ממנו	m'itanu/ mimenu	בשבילנו	bishvilenu	עלינו	alenu	אנחנו
מכם	mkem	בשבילכם	bishvilħem	עליכם	aleħem	אתם
מכן	mken	בשבילכן	bishvilħen	עליכן	aleħen	אתן
מהם	mhem	בשבילם	bishvilam	עליהם	alehem	הם
מהן	mhem	בשבילן	bishvilan	עליהן	alehen	הן

ADDITIONAL_GRAMMAR: 2   דקדוק_נוסף

CONJUGATION OF SOME COMMON VERBS

In this part, conjugation tables of some verbs are listed.

Conjugation of the Verbs for the Past Tense

הם/הן	(אתן)	(אתם)	(אנחנו)	היא	הוא	(את)	(אתה)	(אני)	Inf.
עלו	עליתן	עליתם	עלינו	עלתה	עלה	עלית	עלית	עליתי	לעלות
alu	aliten	alitem	alinu	alta	ala	alit	alita	aliti	la'alot
ענו	עניתן	עניתם	ענינו	ענתה	ענה	ענית	ענית	עניתי	לענות
anu	initen	initem	aninu	anta	ana	anit	anita	aniti	la'anot
עשׂו	עשׂיתן	עשׂיתם	עשׂינו	עשׂתה	עשׂה	עשׂית	עשׂית	עשׂיתי	לעשׂות
asu	asiten	asitem	asinu	asta	asa	asi't	asi'ta	asi'ti	la'asot
עבדו	עבדתן	עבדתם	עבדנו	עבדה	עבד	עבדת	עבדת	עבדתי	לעבוד
avdu	avadten	avadtem	avadnu	avda	avad	avadt	avadta	avadti	la'avod
עזרו	עזרתן	עזרמם	עזרוב	עזרה	עזר	עזרת	עזרת	עזרתי	לעזור
azru	azarten	azartem	azarnu	azra	azar	azart	azarta	azarti	la'azor
עזבו	עזבתן	עזבמם	עזנוב	עזבה	עזב	עזבת	עזבת	עזבתי	לעזוב
azvu	azavten	azavtem	azavnu	azva	azav	azavt	azavta	azavti	la'azov
ידעו	ידעתן	ידעתם	ידענו	ידעה	ידע	ידעת	ידעת	ידעתי	לדעת
yad'u	yda'ten	yda'tem	yada'nu	yad'a	yada	yada't	yada'ta	yada'ti	lada'at

הם/הן	(אתן)	(אתם)	(אנחנו)	היא	הוא	(את)	(אתה)	(אני)	Inf.
גרו	גרתן	גרתם	גרנו	גרה	גר	גרת	גרת	גרתי	לגור
garu	garten	gartem	garnu	gara	gar	gart	garta	garti	lagur
חיכו	חיכיתן	חיכיתם	חיכינו	חיכתה	חיכה	חיכית	חיכית	חיכיתי	לחכות
ħiku	ħikiten	ħikitem	ħikinu	ħikta	ħika	ħikit	ħikita	ħikiti	laħakot
חלמו	חלמתן	חלמתם	חלמנו	חלמה	חלם	חלמת	חלמת	חלמתי	לחלום
ħalmu	ħalamten	ħalamtem	ħalamnu	ħalma	ħalam	ħalamt	ħalamta	ħalamti	laħalom
חשבו	חשבתן	חשבתם	חשבנו	חשבה	חשב	חשבת	חשבת	חשבתי	לחשוב
ħashvu	həshavten	həshavtem	hashavnu	hashva	hashav	hashavt	hashavta	hashavti	laħashov
חזרו	חזרתן	חזרתם	חזרנו	חזרה	חזר	חזרת	חזרת	חזרתי	לחזור
ħazru	ħzarten	ħzartem	ħazarnu	ħazra	ħazar	ħazart	ħazarta	ħazarti	laħazor
לקחו	לקחתן	לקחתם	לקחנו	לקחה	לקח	לקחת	לקחת	לקחתי	לקחת
lakħu	lkaħten	lkaħtem	lakaħnu	lakħa	lakaħ	lakaħt	lakaħta	lakaħti	lakaħat
קמו	קמתן	קמתם	קמנו	קמה	קם	קמת	קמת	קמתי	לקום
kamu	kaktem	kamten	kamnu	kama	kam	kamt	kamta	kamti	lakum
הלכו	הלכתן	הלכתם	הלכנו	הלכה	הלך	הלכת	הלכת	הלכתי	ללכת
halħu	hlaħten	hlaħtem	halaħnu	halħa	halaħ	halaħt	halaħta	halaħti	laleħet
מֵתו	מַתן	מַתם	מַתנו	מֵתה	מֵת	מַתְ	מַתָ	מַתי	למות
metu	maten	matem	matnu	meta	met	mat	mata	mati	lamut
נחו	נחתן	נחתם	נחנו	נחה	נח	נחת	נחת	נחתי	לנוח
naħu	naħten	naħtem	naħnu	naħa	naħ	naħt	naħta	naħti	lanuaħ
ירדו	ירדתן	ירדתם	ירדנו	ירדה	ירד	ירדת	ירדת	ירדתי	לרדת
yardu	yradten	yradtem	yaradnu	yarda	yarad	yaradt	yaradta	yaradti	laredet

הם/הן	(אתן)	(אתם)	(אנחנו)	היא	הוא	(את)	(אתה)	(אני)	Inf.
ישבו	ישבתן	ישבתם	ישבנו	ישבה	ישב	ישבת	ישבת	ישבתי	לשבת
yashvu	yishavten	yishavtem	yashavnu	yashva	yashav	yashavt	yashavta	yashavti	lashevet
שרו	שרתן	שרתם	שרנו	שרה	שר	שרת	שרת	שרתי	לשיר
sharu	sharten	shartem	sharnu	shara	shar	shart	sharta	sharti	lashir
שמו	שמתן	שמתם	שמנו	שמה	שם	שמת	שמת	שמתי	לשים
samu	samten	samtem	samnu	sama	sam	samt	samta	samti	lasim
נתנו	נתתן	נתתם	נתנו	נתנה	נתן	נתת	נתת	נתתי	לתת
natnu	ntaten	ntatem	natannu	natna	natan	natat	natata	natati	latet
טסו	טסתן	טסתם	טסנו	טסה	טס	טסת	טסת	טסתי	לטוס
tasu	tasten	tastem	tasnu	tasa	tas	tast	tasta	tasti	latus
באו	באתן	באתם	באנו	באה	בא	באת	באת	באתי	לבוא
ba'u	ba'ten	ba'tem	ba'nu	ba'a	ba'	ba't	ba'ta	ba'ti	lavo'
אכלו	אכלתן	אכלתם	אכלנו	אכלה	אכל	אכלת	אכלת	אכלתי	לאכול
aḥlu	aḥalten	aḥaltem	aḥalnu	aḥla	aḥal	aḥalt	aḥalta	aḥalti	le'eḥol
אהבו	אהבתן	אהבתם	אהבנו	אהבה	אהב	אהבת	אהבת	אהבתי	לאהוב
ahvu	ahavten	ahavtem	ahavnu	ahva	ahav	ahavt	ahavta	ahavti	le'ehov
דברו	דברתן	דברתם	דברנו	דברה	דבר	דברת	דברת	דברתי	לדבר
dibru	dbarten	dbartem	dibarnu	dibra	diber	dibart	dibarta	dibarti	ledaber
העירו	הערתן	הערתם	הערנו	העירה	העיר	הערת	הערת	הערתי	להעיר
he'iru	he'arten	he'artem	he'arnu	he'ira	he'ir	he'art	he'arta	he'arti	leha'ir
הגיעו	הגעתן	הגעתם	הגענו	הגיעה	הגיע	הגעת	הגעת	הגעתי	להגיע
higi'u	higa'ten	higa'tem	higa'nu	higi'a	higi	higa't	higa'ta	higa'ti	lehagi'a

הם/הן	(אתן)	(אתם)	(אנחנו)	היא	הוא	(את)	(אתה)	(אני)	Inf.
הגידו	הגדתן	הגדתם	הגדנו	הגידה	הגיד	הגדת	הגדת	הגדתי	להגיד
higidu	higadten	higadtem	higadnu	higida	higid	higadt	higadta	higadti	lehagid
הכינו	הכנתן	הכנתם	הכנּו	הכינה	הכין	הכנת	הכנת	הכנתי	להכין
heḥinu	heḥanten	heḥantem	heḥanu	heḥina	heḥin	heḥant	heḥanta	heḥanti	lehaḥin
החליטו	החלטתן	החלטתם	החלטנו	החליטה	החליט	החלטת	החלטת	החלטתי	להחליט
heḥlitu	heḥlatten	heḥlattem	heḥlatnu	heḥlita	heḥlit	heḥlatit	heḥlatta	heḥlatti	lehaḥlit
הכניסו	הכנסתן	הכנסתם	הכנסנו	הכניסה	הכניס	הכנסת	הכנסת	הכנסתי	להכניס
hiḥinsu	hiḥnasten	hiḥnastem	hiḥnasnu	hiḥinsa	hiḥnis	hiḥnast	hiḥnasta	hiḥnasti	lehaḥnis
הכירו	הכרתן	הכרתם	הכרנו	הכירה	הכיר	הכרת	הכרת	הכרתי	להכיר
hikiru	hikarten	hikartem	hikarnu	hikira	hikir	hikart	hikarta	hikarti	lehakir
המתינו	המתנתן	המתנתם	המתנּו	המתינה	המתין	המתנת	המתנת	המתנתי	להמתין
himtinu	himtanten	himtantem	himtannu	himtinu	himtin	himtant	himtanta	himtanti	lehamtin
הרגישו	הרגשתן	הרגשתם	הרגשנו	הרגישה	הרגיש	הרגשת	הרגשת	הרגשתי	להרגיש
hirgishu	hirgashten	hirgashtem	hirgashnu	hirgisha	hirgish	hirgasht	hirgashta	hirgashti	lehargish
הסכימו	הסכמתן	הסכמתם	הסכמנו	הסכימה	הסכים	הסכמת	הסכמת	הסכמתי	להסכים
hiskimu	hiskamten	hiskamtem	hiskamnu	hiskima	hiskim	hiskamt	hiskamta	hiskamti	lehaskim
התאימו	התאמתן	התאמתם	התאמנו	התאימה	התאים	התאמת	התאמת	התאמתי	להתאים
hit'imu	hit'amten	hit'amtem	hit'amnu	hit'ima	hit'im	hit'amt	hit'amta	hit'amti	lehat'im
התחילו	התחלתן	התחלתם	התחלנו	התחילה	התחיל	התחלת	התחלת	התחלתי	להתחיל
hitḥilu	hitḥalten	hitḥaltem	hitḥalnu	hitḥila	hitḥil	hitḥalt	hitḥalta	hitḥalti	lehatḥil
הציעו	הצעתן	הצעתם	הצענו	הציעה	הציע	הצעת	הצעת	הצעתי	להציע
hitsi'u	hitsa'ten	hitsa'tem	hitsa'nu	hitsi'a	hitsi	hitsa't	hitsa'ta	hitsa'ti	lehatsi'a

/הם הן	(אתן)	(אתם)	(אנחנו)	היא	הוא	(את)	(אתה)	(אני)	Inf.
הצליחו	הצלחתן	הצלחתם	הצלחנו	הצליחה	הצליח	הצלחת	הצלחת	הצלחתי	להצליח
hitsliħu	hitslaħten	hitslaħtem	hitslaħnu	hitsliħa	hitsliaħ	hitslaħt	hitslaħta	hitslaħti	lehatsliaħ
הביאו	הבאתן	הבאתם	הבאנו	הביאה	הביא	הראת	הבאת	הבאתי	להביא
hevi'u	heveten	hevetem	hevenu	hevi'a	hevi	hevet	heveta	heveti	lehavi
הבינו	הבנתן	הבנתם	הבנו	הבינה	הבין	הבנת	הבנת	הבנתי	להבין
hevinu	hvanten	hvantem	hevannu	hevina	hevin	hevant	hevanta	hevanti	lehavin
הבריאו	הבראתן	הבראתם	הבראנו	הבריאה	הבריא	הבראת	הבראת	הבראתי	להבריא
hivri'u	hivri'ten	hivri'tem	hivri'nu	hivri'a	hivri	hivri't	hivri'ta	hivri'ti	lehavri
הבטיחו	הבטחתן	הבטחתם	הבטחנו	הבטיחה	הבטיח	הבטחת	הבטחת	הבטחתי	להבטיח
hivti'ħu	hivtaħten	hivtaħtem	hivtaħnu	hivti'ħa	hivti'aħ	hivtaħt	hivtaħta	hivtaħti	lehavti'aħ
הזמינו	הזמנתן	הזמנתם	הזמנו	הזמינה	הזמין	הזמנת	הזמנת	הזמנתי	להזמין
hizminu	hizmanten	hizmantem	hizmanu	hizmina	hizmin	hizmant	hizmanta	hizmanti	lehazmin
נכנסו	נכנסתן	נכנסתם	נכנסנו	נכנסה	נכנס	נכנסת	נכנסת	נכנסתי	להיכנס
niħinsu	niħnasten	niħnastem	niħnasnu	niħinsa	niħnas	niħnast	niħnasta	niħnasti	lehikanes
נפגשו	נפגשתן	נפגשתם	נפגשנו	נפגשה	נפגש	נפגשת	נפגשת	נפגשתי	להיפגש
nifigshu	nifgashten	nifgashtem	nifgashnu	nifigsha	nifgash	nifgasht	nifgashta	nifgashti	lehipagesh
נשארו	נשארתן	נשארתם	נשארנו	נשארה	נשאר	נשארת	נשארת	נשארתי	להישאר
nish'aru	nish'arten	nish'artem	nish'arnu	nish'ara	nish'ar	nish'art	nish'arta	nish'arti	lehisha'er
השתתפו	השתתפתן	השתתפתם	השתתפנו	השתתפה	השתתף	השתתפת	השתתפת	השתתפתי	להשתתף
hishtatfu	hishtataften	hishtataftem	hishtatafnu	hishtatfa	hishtatef	hishtataft	hishtatafta	hishtatafti	lehishtatef
התגעגעו	התגעגעתן	התגעגעתם	התגעגענו	התגעגעה	התגעגע	התגעגעת	התגעגעת	התגעגעתי	להתגעגע
hitga'ig'u	hitga'age'aten	hitga'age'atem	hitga'age'anu	hitga'ig'a	hitga'age'a	hitga'age'at	hitga'age'ata	hitga'age'ati	lehitga'age'a

הם/הן	(אתן)	(אתם)	(אנחנו)	היא	הוא	(את)	(אתה)	(אני)	Inf.
התחתנו	התחתנתן	התחתנתם	התחתנו	התחתנה	התחתן	התחתנת	התחתנת	התחתנתי	להתחתן
hitħatnu	*hitħatenten*	*hitħatentem*	*hitħatennu*	*hitħatna*	*hitħaten*	*hitħatent*	*hitħatenta*	*hitħatenti*	*lehitħaten*
התעוררו	התעוררתן	התעוררתם	התעוררנו	התעוררה	התעורר	התעוררת	התעוררת	התעוררתי	להתעורר
hit'torru	*hit'orerten*	*hit'orertem*	*nit'orernu*	*hit'orra*	*hit'orer*	*hit'orert*	*hit'orerta*	*hit'orerti*	*lehit'orer*
התפללו	התפללתן	התפללתם	התפללנו	התפללה	התפלל	התפללת	התפללת	התפללתי	להתפלל
hitpallu	*hitpalelten*	*hitpaleltem*	*hitpalelnu*	*hitpalla*	*hitpalel*	*hitpalelt*	*hitpalelta*	*hitpalelti*	*lehitpalel*
התרגלו	התרגלתן	התרגלתם	התרגלנו	התרגלה	התרגל	התרגלת	התרגלת	התרגלתי	להתרגל
hitraglu	*hitragelten*	*hitrageltem*	*hitragelnu*	*hitragla*	*hitragel*	*hitragelt*	*hitragelta*	*hitragelti*	*lehitragel*
התרגשו	התרגשתן	התרגשתם	התרגשנו	התרגשה	התרגש	התרגשת	התרגשת	התרגשתי	להתרגש
hitragshu	*hitrageshten*	*hitrageshtem*	*hitrageshnu*	*hitragsha*	*hitragesh*	*hitragesht*	*hitrageshta*	*hitrageshti*	*lehitragesh*
התרחצו	התרחצתן	התרחצתם	התרחצנו	התרחצה	התרחץ	התרחצת	התרחצת	התרחצתי	להתרחץ
hitraħtsu	*hitraħetsten*	*hitraħetstem*	*hitraħetsnu*	*hitraħtsa*	*hitraħets*	*hitraħetst*	*hitraħetsta*	*hitraħetsti*	*lehitraħets*
התקשרו	התקשרתן	התקשרתם	התקשרנו	התקשרה	התקשר	התקשרת	התקשרת	התקשרתי	להתקשר
hitkashru	*hitkasherten*	*hitkashertem*	*hitkashernu*	*hitkashra*	*hitkasher*	*hitkashert*	*hitkasherta*	*hitkasherti*	*lehitkasher*
הצטערו	הצטערתן	הצטערתם	הצטערנו	הצטערה	הצטער	הצטערת	הצטערת	הצטערתי	להצטער
hitsta'ru	*hitsta'erten*	*hitsta'ertem*	*hitsta'ernu*	*hitsta'ra*	*hitsta'er*	*hitsta'ert*	*hitsta'erta*	*hitsta'erti*	*lehitsta'er*
הוציאו	הוציאתן	הוציאתם	הוציאנו	הוציאה	הוציא	הוציאת	הוציאת	הוציאתי	להוציא
hotsi'u	*hotse'ten*	*hotse'tem*	*hotse'nu*	*hotsi'a*	*hotsi'*	*hotse't*	*hotse'ta*	*hotse'ti*	*lehotsi*
קיבלו	קיבלתן	קיבלתם	קיבלנו	קיבלה	קיבל	קיבלת	קיבלת	קיבלתי	לקבל
kiblu	*kibalten*	*kibaltem*	*kibalnu*	*kibla*	*kibel*	*kibalt*	*kibalta*	*kibalti*	*lekabel*
ניגנו	ניגנתן	ניגנתם	ניגנו	ניגנה	ניגן	ניגנת	ניגנת	ניגנתי	לנגן
nignu	*niganten*	*nigantem*	*nigannu*	*nigna*	*nigen*	*nigant*	*niganta*	*niganti*	*lenagen*

הם/הן	(אתן)	(אתם)	(אנחנו)	היא	הוא	(את)	(אתה)	(אני)	Inf.
ניקו	ניקיתן	ניקיתם	ניקינו	ניקתה	ניקה	ניקית	ניקית	ניקיתי	לנקות
niku	nikiten	nikitem	nikinu	nikta	nika	nikit	nikita	nikiti	lenakot
ריפאו	ריפאתן	ריפאתם	ריפאנו	ריפאה	ריפא	ריפאת	ריפאת	ריפאתי	לרפא
rip'u	ripe'ten	ripe'tem	ripe'nu	rip'e	ripe	ripe't	ripe'ta	ripe'ti	lerape
סידרו	סידרתן	סידרתם	סידרנו	סידרה	סידר	סידרת	סידרת	סידרתי	לסדר
sidru	sidarten	sidartem	sidarnu	sidra	sider	sidart	sidarta	sidarti	lesader
סיימו	סיימתן	סיימתם	סיימנו	סיימה	סיים	סיימת	סיימת	סיימתי	לסיים
siymu	siyamten	siyamtem	siyamnu	siyma	siyem	siyamt	siyamta	siyamti	lesayem
שילמו	שילמתן	שילמתם	שילמנו	שילמה	שילם	שילמת	שילמת	שילמתי	לשלם
shilmu	shilamten	shilamtem	shilamnu	shilma	shilem	shilamt	shilamta	shilamti	leshalem
טיילו	טיילתן	טיילתם	טיילנו	טיילה	טייל	טיילת	טיילת	טיילתי	לטייל
tiylu	tiyalten	tiyaltem	tiyalnu	tiyla	tiyel	tiyalt	tiyalta	tiyalti	letayel
ביקרו	ביקרתן	ביקרתם	ביקרנו	ביקרה	ביקר	ביקרת	ביקרת	ביקרתי	לבקר
bikru	bkarten	bkartem	bikarnu	bikra	biker	bikart	bikarta	bikarti	levaker
ביקשו	ביקשתן	ביקשתם	ביקשנו	ביקשה	ביקש	ביקשת	ביקשת	ביקשתי	לבקש
bikshu	bikashten	bikashtem	bikashnu	biksha	bikesh	bikasht	bikashta	bikashti	levakesh
בישלו	בישלתן	בישלתם	בישלנו	בישלה	בישל	בישלת	בישלת	בישלתי	לבשל
bishlu	bishalten	bishaltem	bishalnu	bishla	bishel	bishalt	bishalta	bishalti	levashel
פגשו	פגשתן	פגשתם	פגשנו	פגשה	פגש	פגשת	פגשת	פגשתי	לפגוש
pagshu	pgashten	pgashtem	pagashnu	pagsha	pagash	pagasht	pagashta	pagashti	lifgosh
פחדו	פחדתן	פחדתם	פחדנו	פחדה	פחד	פחדת	פחדת	פחדתי	לפחוד
paħdu	paħadten	paħadtem	paħadnu	paħda	paħad	paħadt	paħadta	paħadti	lifhod

הם/הן	(אתן)	(אתם)	(אנחנו)	היא	הוא	(את)	(אתה)	(אני)	Inf.
כאבו	כאבתן	כאבתם	כאבנו	כאבה	כאב	כאבת	כאבתָ	כאבתי	לכאוב
ka'vu	ka'avten	ka'avtem	ka'avnu	ka'va	ka'av	ka'avt	ka'avta	ka'avti	liħ'ov
כתבו	כתבתן	כתבתם	כתבנו	כתבה	כתב	כתבת	כתבתָ	כתבתי	לכתוב
katvu	ktavten	ktavtem	katavnu	katva	katav	katavt	katavta	katavti	liħtov
קנו	קניתן	קניתם	קנינו	קנתה	קנה	קנית	קניתָ	קניתי	לקנות
kanu	kaniten	kanitem	kaninu	kanta	kana	kanit	kanita	kaniti	liknot
קראו	קראתן	קראתם	קראנו	קראה	קרא	קראת	קראתָ	קראתי	לקרוא
kar'u	kra'ten	kra'tem	kara'nu	kar'a	kara'	kara't	kara'ta	kara'ti	likro'
לבשו	לבשתן	לבשתם	לבשנו	לבשה	לבש	לבשת	לבשתָ	לבשתי	ללבוש
lavshu	lavashten	lavashtem	lavashnu	lavsha	lavash	lavasht	lavashta	lavashti	lilbosh
למדתו	למדתן	למדתם	למדנו	למדה	למד	למדת	למדתָ	למדתי	ללמוד
lamdu	lmadten	lmadtem	lamadnu	lamda	lamad	lamadt	lamadta	lamadti	lilmod
מכרו	מכרתן	מכרתם	מכרנו	מכרה	מכר	מכרת	מכרתָ	מכרתי	למכור
maħru	mħarten	mħartem	maħarnu	maħra	maħar	maħart	maħarta	maħarti	limkor
מצאו	מצאתן	מצאתם	מצאנו	מצאה	מצא	מצאת	מצאתָ	מצאתי	למצוא
mats'u	matsa'ten	matsa'tem	matsa'nu	mats'a	matsa	matsa't	matsa'ta	matsa'ti	limtso
נהגו	נהגתן	נהגתם	נהגנו	נהגה	נהג	נהגת	נהגתָ	נהגתי	לנהוג
nahgu	nahagten	nahagtem	nahagnu	nahga	nahag	nahagt	nahagta	nahagti	linhog
נסעו	נסעתן	נסעתם	נסענו	נסעה	נסע	נסעת	נסעתָ	נסעתי	לנסוע
nas'u	nsa'ten	nsa'tem	nasa'nu	nas'a	nasa	nasa't	nasa'ta	nasa'ti	linso'a
ראו	ראיתן	ראיתם	ראינו	ראתה	ראה	ראית	ראיתָ	ראיתי	לראות
ra'u	ri'iten	ri'item	ra'inu	ra'ta	ra'a	ra'it	ra'ita	ra'iti	lir'ot

הם/הן	(אתן)	(אתם)	(אנחנו)	היא	הוא	(את)	(אתה)	(אני)	Inf.
רקדו	רקדתן	רקדתם	רקדנו	רקדה	רקד	רקדתְּ	רקדתָ	רקדתי	לרקוד
rakdu	*rakadten*	*rakadtem*	*rakadnu*	*rakda*	*rakad*	*rakadt*	*rakadta*	*rakadti*	*lirkod*
רשמו	רשמתן	רשמתם	רשמנו	רשמה	רשַם	רשַמתְּ	רשַמתָ	רשמתי	לרשום
rashmu	*rashamten*	*rashamtem*	*rashamnu*	*rashma*	*rasham*	*rashamt*	*rashamta*	*rashamti*	*lirshom*
רצו	רציתן	רציתם	רצינו	רצתה	רצה	רצִיתְ	רצִיתָ	רציתי	לרצות
ratsu	*ritsiten*	*ritsitem*	*ratsinu*	*ratsta*	*ratsa*	*ratsit*	*ratsita*	*ratsiti*	*lirtsot*
שאלו	שאלתן	שאלתם	שאלנו	שאלה	שאל	שאלתְ	שאלתָ	שאלתי	לשאול
sha'lu	*sha'alten*	*sha'altem*	*sha'alnu*	*sha'la*	*sha'al*	*sha'alt*	*sha'alta*	*sha'alti*	*lish'ol*
שכחו	שכחתן	שכחתם	שכחנו	שכחה	שכח	שכחתְּ	שכחתָ	שכחתי	לשכוח
shaħħu	*shaħaħten*	*shaħaħtem*	*shaħaħnu*	*shaħħa*	*shaħaħ*	*shaħaħt*	*shaħaħta*	*shaħaħti*	*lishko'aħ*
שלחו	שלחתן	שלחתם	שלחנו	שלחה	שלח	שלחתְּ	שלחתָ	שלחתי	לשלוח
shalħu	*shalaħten*	*shalaħtem*	*shalaħnu*	*shalħa*	*shalaħ*	*shalaħt*	*shalaħta*	*shalaħti*	*lishlo'aħ*
שמעו	שמעתן	שמעתם	שמענו	שמעה	שמע	שמעתְּ	שמעתָ	שמעתי	לשמוע
sham'u	*shma'ten*	*shma'tem*	*shma'nu*	*sham'a*	*shama*	*shama't*	*shama'ta*	*shama'ti*	*lishmo'a*
ישנו	ישנתן	ישנתם	ישנּו	ישנה	ישן	ישַנתָּ	ישַנתָ	ישנתי	לישון
yashnu	*yashanten*	*yashantem*	*yashannu*	*yashna*	*yashan*	*yashant*	*yashanta*	*yashanti*	*lishon*
שחו	שחיתן	שחיתם	שחינו	שחתה	שחה	שחִיתָ	שחִיתָ	שחיתי	לשחות
saħu	*shiten*	*shitem*	*saħinu*	*saħta*	*saħa*	*saħit*	*saħita*	*saħiti*	*lishot*
שתו	שתיתן	שתיתם	שתינו	שתתה	שתה	שתִיתָ	שתִיתָ	שתיתי	לשתות
shatu	*shtiten*	*shtitem*	*shatinu*	*shatta*	*shata*	*shatit*	*shatita*	*shatiti*	*lishtot*
שכרו	שכרתן	שכרתם	שכרנו	שכרה	שכר	שכרתָּ	שכרתָ	שכרתי	לשכור
saħru	*sharten*	*shartem*	*saħarnu*	*saħra*	*saħar*	*saħart*	*saħarta*	*saħarti*	*liskor*

הם/הן	(אתן)	(אתם)	(אנחנו)	היא	הוא	(את)	(אתה)	(אני)	Inf.
בדקו	בדקתן	בדקתם	בדקנו	בדקה	בדק	בדקְתְ	בדקְתָ	בדקתי	לבדוק
badku	badakten	badaktem	badaknu	badka	badak	badakt	badakta	badakti	livdok
אמרו	אמרתן	אמרתם	אמרנו	אמרה	אמר	אמרְתְ	אמרְתָ	אמרתי	לומר\לאמור
amru	amarten	amartem	amarnu	amra	amar	amart	amarta	amarti	lomar

Note: The subject pronouns in the brackets do not have to be used with the verb.

Conjugation of the Verbs for the Present Tense

הוא	(את)	(אתה)	(אני)	infinitive
עוֹלוֹת	עוֹלִים	עוֹלָה	עוֹלֶה	לַעֲלוֹת
olot	olim	ola	ole	la'alot
עוֹנוֹת	עוֹנִים	עוֹנָה	עוֹנֶה	לַעֲנוֹת
onot	onim	ona	one	la'anot
עוֹשׂוֹת	עוֹשִׂים	עוֹשָׂה	עוֹשֶׂה	לַעֲשׂוֹת
osot	osim	osa	ose	la'asot
עוֹבְדוֹת	עוֹבְדִים	עוֹבֶדֶת	עוֹבֵד	לַעֲבוֹד
ovdot	ovdim	ovedet	oved	la'avod
עוֹזְרוֹת	עוֹזְרִים	עוֹזֶרֶת	עוֹרֵב	לַעֲזוֹר
ozrot	ozrim	ozeret	ozer	la'azov
עוֹזְבוֹת	עוֹזְבִים	עוֹזֶבֶת	עוֹזֵב	לַעֲזוֹב
ozvot	ozvim	ozevet	ozev	la'azov
יוֹדְעוֹת	יוֹדְעִים	יוֹדַעַת	יוֹדֵעַ	לָדַעַת
yod'ot	yod'im	yoda'at	yode'a	lada'at
גָּרוֹת	גָּרִים	גָּרָה	גָּר	לָגוּר
garot	garim	gara	gar	lagur
מְחַכּוֹת	מְחַכִּים	מְחַכָּה	מְחַכֶּה	לְחַכּוֹת
mħakot	mħakim	meħaka	meħake	laħakot

הוא	(את)	(אתה)	(אני)	infinitive
חולמות	חולמים	חולמת	חולם	לחלום
ħolemot	ħolemim	ħolemet	ħolem	laħalom
חושבות	חושבים	חושבת	חושב	לחשוב
ħoshvot	ħoshvim	ħoshevet	ħoshev	laħashov
חוזרות	חוזרים	חוזרת	חוזר	לחזור
ħozrot	ħozrim	ħozeret	ħozer	laħazor
לוקחות	לוקחים	לוקחת	לוקח	לקחת
lokħot	lokħim	lokaħat	loke'aħ	lakaħat
קמות	קמים	קמה	קם	לקום
kamot	kamim	kama	kam	lakum
הולכות	הולכים	הולכת	הולך	ללכת
holħot	holħim	holeħet	holeħ	laleħet
מתות	מתים	מתה	מת	למות
metot	metim	meta	met	lamut
נחות	נחים	נחה	נח	לנוח
naħot	naħim	naħa	naħ	lanuaħ
יורדות	יורדים	יורדת	יורד	לרדת
yordot	yordim	yoredet	yored	laredet
יושבות	יושבים	יושבת	יושב	לשבת
yoshvot	yoshvim	yoshevet	yoshev	lashevet

הוא	(את)	(אתה)	(אני)	infinitive
שרות	שרים	שרה	שר	לשיר
sharot	sharim	shara	shar	lashir
שׂמות	שׂמים	שׂמה	שׂם	לשים
samot	samim	sama	sam	lasim
נותנות	נותנים	נותנת	נותן	לתת
notnot	notnim	notenet	noten	latet
טסות	טסים	טסה	טס	לטוס
tasot	tasim	tasa	tas	latus
באות	באים	באה	בא	לבוא
ba'ot	ba'im	ba'a	ba	lavo'
אוכלות	אוכלים	אוכלת	אוכל	לאכול
oħlot	oħlim	oħelet	oħel	le'eħol
אוהבות	אוהבים	אוהבת	אוהב	לאהוב
ohavot	ohavim	ohevet	ohev	le'ehov
מדברות	מדברים	מדברת	מדבר	לדבר
medabrot	medabrim	medaberet	medaber	ledaber
מעירות	מעירים	מעירה	מעיר	להעיר
me'irot	me'irim	me'ira	me'ir	leha'ir
מגיעות	מגיעים	מגיעה	מגיע	להגיע
megi'ot	megi'im	mgi'a	megi'a	lehagi'a

הוא	(את)	(אתה)	(אני)	infinitive
מגידות	מגידים	מגידה	מגיד	להגיד
magidot	magidim	magida	magid	lehagid
מכינות	מכינים	מכינה	מכין	להכין
meḥinot	meḥinim	meḥina	meḥin	lehaḥin
מחליטות	מחליטים	מחליטה	מחליט	להחליט
maḥlitot	maḥlitim	maḥlita	maḥlit	lehaḥlit
מכניסות	מכניסים	מכניסה	מכניס	להכניס
maḥnisot	maḥnisim	maḥnisa	maḥnis	lehaḥnis
מכירות	מכירים	מכירה	מכיר	להכיר
makirot	makirim	makira	makir	lehakir
ממתינות	ממתינים	ממתינה	ממתין	להמתין
mamtinot	mamtinim	mamtina	mamtin	lehamtin
מרגישות	מרגישים	מרגישה	מרגיש	להרגיש
margishot	margishim	margisha	margish	lehargish
מסכימות	מסכימים	מסכימה	מסכים	להסכים
maskimot	maskimim	maskima	maskim	lehaskim
מתאימות	מתאימים	מתאימה	מתאים	להתאים
mat'imot	mat'imim	mat'ima	mat'im	lehat'im
מתחילות	מתחילים	מתחילה	מתחיל	להתחיל
matḥilot	matḥilim	matḥila	matḥil	lehatḥil

הוא	(את)	(אתה)	(אני)	infinitive
מציעות	מציעים	מציעה	מציע	להציע
matsi'ot	matsi'im	matsi'ya	matsi'a	lehatsi'a
מצליחות	מצליחים	מצליחה	מצליח	להצליח
matsliħot	matsliħim	matsliħa	matsliaħ	lehatsliaħ
מביאות	מביאים	מביאה	מביא	להביא
mevi'ot	mevi'im	mevi'a	mevi	lehavi
מבינות	מבינים	מבינה	מבין	להבין
mvinot	mvinim	mevina	mevin	lehavin
מבריאות	מבריאים	מבריאה	מבריא	להבריא
mavri'ot	mavri'im	mavri'a	mavri	lehavri
מבטיחות	מבטיחים	מבטיחה	מבטיח	להבטיח
mavti'ħot	mavti'ħim	mavti'ħa	mavti'aħ	lehavti'aħ
מזמינות	מזמינים	מזמינה	מזמין	להזמין
mazminot	mazminim	mazmina	mazmin	lehazmin
נכנסות	נכנסים	נכנסת	נכנס	להיכנס
niħnasot	niħnasim	niħneset	niħnas	lehikanes
נפגשות	נפגשים	נפגשת	נפגש	להיפגש
nifgasho	nifgashim	nifgeshet	nifgash	lehipagesh

infinitive	(אני)	(אתה)	(את)	הוא
להישאר	נשאר	נשארת	נשארים	נשארות
lehisha'er	nish'ar	nish'eret	nish'aim	nish'arot
להשתתף	משתתף	משתתפת	משתתפים	משתתפות
lehishtatef	mishtatef	mishtatefet	mishtatfim	mishtatfot
להתגעגע	מתגעגע	מתגעגעת	מתגעגעים	מתגעגעות
lehitga'age'a	mitga'age'a	mitga'age'at	mitga'age'im	mitga'age'ot
להתחתן	מתחתן	מתחתנת	מתחתנים	מתחתנות
lehithaten	mithaten	mithatenet	mithatnim	mithatnot
להתעורר	מתעורר	מתעוררת	מתעוררים	מתעוררות
lehitorer	mitorer	mitoreret	mit'orrim	mit'orrot
להתפלל	מתפלל	מתפללת	מתפללים	מתפללות
lehitpalel	mitpalel	mitpalelet	mitpallim	mitpallot
להתרגל	מתרגל	מתרגלת	מתרגלים	מתרגלות
lehitragel	mitragel	mitragelet	mitraglim	mitraglot
להתרגש	מתרגש	מתרגשת	מתרגשים	מתרגשות
lehitragesh	mitragesh	mitrageshet	mitragshim	mitragshot
להתרחץ	מתרחץ	מתרחצת	מתרחצים	מתרחצות
lehitrahets	mitrahets	mitrahetset	mitrahetsim	mitrahetsot
להתקשר	מתקשר	מתקשרת	מתקשרים	מתקשרות
lehitkasher	mitkasher	mitkaskeret	mitkashrim	mitkashrot

הוא	(את)	(אתה)	(אני)	infinitive
מצטערות	מצטערים	מצטערת	מצטער	להצטער
mitsta'rot	mitsta'rim	mitsta'eret	mitsta'er	lehitsta'er
מוציאות	מוציאים	מוציאה	מוציא	להוציא
motsi'ot	motsi'im	motsi'a	motsi	lehotsi
מקבלות	מקבלים	מקבלת	מקבל	לקבל
mekablot	mekablim	mekabelet	mekabel	lekabel
מנגנות	מנגנים	מנגנת	מנגן	לנגן
mnagnot	mnagnim	mnagenet	mnagen	lenagen
מנקות	מנקים	מנקָה	מנקֶה	לנקות
mnakot	mnakim	mnaka	menake	lenakot
מרפאות	מרפאים	מרפאת	מרפא	לרפא
merap'ot	merap'im	merapet	merape	lerape
מסדרות	מסדרים	מסדרת	מסדר	לסדר
mesadrot	mesadrim	mesaderet	mesader	lesader
מסיימות	מסיימים	מסיימת	מסיים	לסיים
msayemot	msayemim	msayemet	msayem	lesayem
משלמות	משלמים	משלמת	משלם	לשלם
mshalmot	mshalmim	mshalemet	mshalem	leshalem
מטיילות	מטיילים	מטיילת	מטייל	לטייל
metaylot	metaylim	metayelet	metayel	letayel

הוא	(את)	(אתה)	(אני)	infinitive
מבקרות	מבקרים	מבקרת	מבקר	לבקר
mevakrot	*mevakrim*	*mevakeret*	*mevaker*	*levaker*
מבקשות	מבקשים	מבקשת	מבקש	לבקש
mevakshot	*mevakshim*	*mevakeshet*	*mevakesh*	*levakesh*
מבשלות	מבשלים	מבשלת	מבשל	לבשל
mevashlot	*mevashlim*	*mevashelet*	*mevashel*	*levashel*
פוגשות	פוגשים	פוגשת	פוגש	לפגוש
pogsho	*pogshim*	*pogeshet*	*pogesh*	*lifgosh*
פוחדות	פוחדים	פוחדת	פוחד	לפחוד
poħdot	*poħdim*	*poħedet*	*poħed*	*lifħod*
כואבות	כואבים	כואבת	כואב	לכאוב
ko'vot	*ko'vim*	*ko'evet*	*ko'ev*	*liħ'ov*
כותבות	כותבים	כותבת	כותב	לכתוב
kotvot	*kotvim*	*kotevet*	*kotev*	*liħtov*
קונות	קונים	קונָה	קונֶה	לקנות
konot	*konim*	*kona*	*kone*	*liknot*
קוראות	קוראים	קוראת	קורא	לקרוא
korot	*korim*	*koret*	*kore*	*likro'*
לובשות	לובשים	לובשת	לובש	ללבוש
lovshot	*lovshim*	*loveshet*	*lovesh*	*lilbosh*

infinitive	(אני)	(אתה)	(את)	הוא
ללמוד	לומד	לומדת	לומדים	לומדות
lilmod	lomed	lomede	lomdim	lomdot
למכור	מוכר	מוכרת	מוכרים	מוכרות
limkor	moker	mokeret	mokrim	mokrot
למצוא	מוצא	מוצאת	מוצאים	מוצאות
limtso	motse	motset	motsim	motsot
לנהוג	נוהג	נוהגת	נוהגים	נוהגות
linhog	noheg	noheget	nohagim	nohagot
לנסוע	נוסע	נוסעת	נוסעים	נוסעות
linso'a	nose'a	nosa'at	nos'im	nos'ot
לראות	רוֹאֶה	רוֹאָה	רואים	רואות
lir'ot	ro'e	ro'a	ro'im	ro'ot
לרקוד	רוקד	רוקדת	רוקדים	רוקדות
lirkod	roked	rokedet	rokdim	rokdot
לרשום	רושם	רושמת	רושמים	רושמות
lirshom	roshem	roshemet	roshmim	rohmot
לרצות	רוֹצֶה	רוֹצָה	רוצים	רוצות
lirtsot	rotse	rotsa	rotsim	rotsot
לשאול	שואל	שואלת	שואלים	שואלות
lish'ol	sho'el	sho'elet	sho'lim	sho'lot

הוא	(את)	(אתה)	(אני)	infinitive
שוכחות	שוכחים	שוכחת	שוכח	לשכוח
shoħħot	*shoħħim*	*shoħaħat*	*shoħeħ*	*lishko'aħ*
שולחות	שולחים	שולחת	שולח	לשלוח
sholħot	*sholħim*	*shole'ħat*	*shole'aħ*	*lishlo'aħ*
שומעות	שומעים	שומעת	שומע	לשמוע
shom'ot	*shom'im*	*shoma'at*	*shome'a*	*lishmo'a*
ישנות	ישנים	ישנה	ישן	לישון
yashenot	*yashenim*	*yashena*	*yashen*	*lishon*
שׂוחות	שׂוחים	שׂוחה	שׂוחה	לשׂחות
soħot	*soħim*	*soħa*	*soħe*	*lisħot*
שותות	שותים	שותה	שותה	לשתות
shotot	*shotim*	*shota*	*shote*	*lishtot*
שׂוכרות	שׂוכרים	שׂוכרת	שׂוכר	לשׂכור
soħrot	*soħrim*	*soħeret*	*soħer*	*liskor*
בודקות	בודקים	בודקת	בודק	לבדוק
bodkot	*bodkim*	*bodeket*	*bodek*	*livdok*
אומרות	אומרים	אומרת	אומר	לומר\לאמור
omrot	*omrim*	*omeret*	*omer*	*lomar*

Conjugation of the Verbs for the Future Tense

הם / הן	(אתן) / (אתם)	(אנחנו)	היא	הוא	(את)	(אתה)	(אני)	Inf.
יעלו	תעלו	נעלה	תעלה	יעלה	תעלי	תעלה	אעלה	לעלות
ya'alu	ta'alu	na'ale	ta'ale	ya'ale	ta'ali	ta'ale	e'ele	la'alot
יענו	תענו	נענה	תענה	יענה	תעני	תענה	אענה	לענות
ya'anu	ta'anu	na'ane	ta'ane	ya'ane	ta'ani	ta'ane	e'ene	la'anot
יעשׂו	תעשׂו	נעשׂה	תעשׂה	יעשׂה	תעשׂי	תעשׂה	אעשׂה	לעשׂות
ya'asu	ta'asu	ne'ase	ta'ase	ye'ase	ta'asi	ta'ase	e'ase	la'asot
יעבדו	תעבדו	נעבוד	תעבוד	יעבוד	תעבדי	תעבוד	אעבוד	לעבוד
ya'avdu	ta'avdu	na'avod	ta'avod	ya'avod	ta'avdi	ta'avod	e'evod	la'avod
יעזרו	תעזרו	נעזור	תעזור	יעזור	תעזרי	תעזור	אעזור	לעזור
ya'azru	ta'azru	na'ezor	ta'ezor	ya'ezor	ta'azri	ta'ezor	e'ezor	la'azor
יעזבו	תעזבו	נעזוב	תעזוב	יעזוב	תעזבי	תעזוב	אעזוב	לעזוב
ya'azvu	ta'azvu	na'ezov	ta'ezov	ya'ezov	ta'azvi	ta'ezov	e'ezov	la'azov
ידעו	תדעו	נדע	תדע	ידע	תדעי	תדע	אדע	לדעת
yed'u	ted'u	neda	teda	yeda	ted'i	teda	eda	lada'at
יגורו	תגורו	נגור	תגור	יגור	תגורי	תגור	אגור	לגור
yaguru	taguru	nagur	tagur	yagur	taguri	tagur	agur	lagur
יחכו	תחכו	נחכה	תחכה	יחכה	תחכי	תחכה	אחכה	לחכות
yiḥaku	tiḥaku	niḥake	tiḥake	yiḥake	tiḥaki	tiḥake	eḥake	laḥakot
יחלמו	תחלמו	נחלום	תחלום	יחלום	תחלמי	תחלום	אחלום	לחלום
yaḥalmu	taḥalmu	naḥalom	taḥalom	yaḥalom	taḥalmi	taḥalom	eḥalom	laḥalom

הם / הן	(אתן) / (אתם)	(אנחנו)	היא	הוא	(את)	(אתה)	(אני)	Inf.
יחשבו	תחשבו	נחשוב	תחשוב	יחשוב	תחשבי	תחשוב	אחשוב	לחשוב
yaħashvu	*taħashvu*	*naħshov*	*taħshov*	*yaħshov*	*taħashvi*	*taħshov*	*eħshov*	*laħashov*
יחזרו	תחזרו	נחזור	תחזור	יחזור	תחזרי	תחזור	אחזור	לחזור
yaħazru	*taħazru*	*naħazor*	*taħazor*	*yaħazor*	*taħazri*	*taħazor*	*eħezor*	*laħazor*
יקחו	תקחו	נקח	תקח	יקח	תקחי	תקח	אקח	לקחת
yikħu	*tikħu*	*nikaħ*	*tikaħ*	*yikaħ*	*tikħi*	*tikaħ*	*ekaħ*	*lakaħat*
יקומו	תקומו	נקום	תקום	יקום	תקומי	תקום	אקום	לקום
yakumu	*takumu*	*nakum*	*takum*	*yakum*	*takumi*	*takum*	*akum*	*lakum*
ילכו	תלכו	נלך	תלך	ילך	תלכי	תלך	אלך	ללכת
yelħu	*telħu*	*neleħ*	*teleħ*	*yeleħ*	*telħi*	*teleħ*	*eleħ*	*laleħet*
ימותו	תמותו	נמות	תמות	ימות	תמותי	תמות	אמות	למות
yamudu	*tamudu*	*namut*	*tamut*	*yamut*	*tamuti*	*tamut*	*amut*	*lamut*
ינוחו	תנוחו	ננוח	תנוח	ינוח	תנוחי	תנוח	אנוח	לנוח
yanuħu	*tanuħu*	*nanu'aħ*	*tanu'aħ*	*yanu'aħ*	*tanuħi*	*tanu'aħ*	*anu'aħ*	*lanu'aħ*
ירדו	תרדו	נרד	תרד	ירד	תרדי	תרד	ארד	לרדת
yerdu	*terdu*	*nered*	*tered*	*yered*	*terdi*	*tered*	*ered*	*laredet*
ישבו	תשבו	נשב	תשב	ישב	תשבי	תשב	אשב	לשבת
yeshvu	*teshvu*	*neshev*	*teshev*	*yeshev*	*teshvi*	*teshev*	*eshev*	*lashevet*
ישירו	תשירו	נשיר	תשיר	ישיר	תשירי	תשיר	אשיר	לשיר
yashiru	*tashiru*	*nashir*	*tashir*	*yashir*	*tashiri*	*tashir*	*ashir*	*lashir*
ישימו	תשימו	נשים	תשים	ישים	תשימי	תשים	אשים	לשים
yasimu	*tasimu*	*nasim*	*tasim*	*yasim*	*tasimi*	*tasim*	*asim*	*lasim*

Inf.	(אני)	(אתה)	(את)	הוא	היא	(אנחנו)	(אתן) / (אתם)	הם / הן
לטוס	אטוס	תטוס	תטוסי	יטוס	תטוס	נטוס	תטוסו	יטוסו
latus	atus	tatus	tatusi	yatus	tatus	natus	tatusu	yatusu
לתת	אתן	תיתן	תיתני	ייתן	תיתן	ניתן	תיתנו	ייתנו
latet	eten	titen	titni	yiten	titen	niten	titnu	yitnu
לבוא	אבוא	תבוא	תבואי	יבוא	תבוא	נבוא	תבואו	יבואו
lavo'	avo	tavo	tavo'i	yavo	tavo	navo	tavo'u	yavo'u
לאכול	אוכל	תאכל	תאכלי	יאכל	תאכל	נאכל	תאכלו	יאכלו
le'eħol	oħal	toħal	toħli	yoħal	toħal	noħal	toħlu	yoħlu
לאהוב	אוהב	תאהב	תאהבי	יאהב	תאהב	נאהב	תאהבו	יאהבו
le'ehov	ohav	tohav	tohavi	yohav	tohav	nohav	tohavu	yohavu
לדבר	אדבר	תדבר	תדברי	ידבר	תדבר	נדבר	תדברו	ידברו
ledaber	edaber	tidaber	tidabri	yidaber	tidaber	nidaber	tidabru	yidabru
להעיר	אעיר	תעיר	תעירי	יעיר	תעיר	נעיר	תעירו	יעירו
leha'ir	a'ir	ta'ir	ta'iri	ya'ir	ta'ir	na'ir	ta'iru	ya'ir
להגיע	אגיע	תגיע	תגיעי	יגיע	תגיע	נגיע	תגיעו	יגיעו
lehagi'a	agi'a	tagi'a	tagi'i	yagi'a	tagi'a	nagi'a	tagi'u	yagi'u
להגיד	אגיד	תגיד	תגידי	יגיד	תגיד	נגיד	תגידו	יגידו
lehagid	agid	tagid	tagidi	yagid	tagid	nagid	tagidu	yagidu
להכין	אכין	תכין	תכיני	יכין	תכין	נכין	תכינו	יכינו
lehaħin	aħin	taħin	taħini	yaħin	taħin	naħin	taħinu	yaħinu
להחליט	אחליט	תחליט	תחליטי	יחליט	תחליט	נחליט	תחליטו	יחליטו
lehaħlit	aħlit	taħlit	taħliti	yaħlit	taħlit	naħlit	taħlitu	yaħlitu

הם / הן	(אתן) / (אתם)	(אנחנו)	היא	הוא	(את)	(אתה)	(אני)	Inf.
יכניסו	תכניסו	נכניס	תכניס	יכניס	תכניסי	תכניס	אכניס	להכניס
yaħnisu	*taħnisu*	*naħnis*	*taħnis*	*yaħnis*	*taħnisi*	*taħnis*	*aħnis*	*lehaħnis*
יכירו	תכירו	נכיר	תכיר	יכיר	תכירי	תכיר	אכיר	להכיר
yakiru	*takiru*	*nakir*	*takir*	*yakir*	*takiri*	*takir*	*akir*	*lehakir*
ימתינו	תמתינו	נמתין	תמתין	ימתין	תמתיני	תמתין	אמתין	להמתין
yamtinu	*tamtinu*	*namtin*	*tamtin*	*yamtin*	*tamtini*	*tamtin*	*amtin*	*lehamtin*
ירגישו	תרגישו	נרגיש	תרגיש	ירגיש	תרגישי	תרגיש	ארגיש	להרגיש
yargishu	*targishu*	*nargish*	*targish*	*yargish*	*targishi*	*targish*	*argish*	*lehargish*
יסכימו	תסכימו	נסכים	תסכים	יסכים	תסכימי	תסכים	אסכים	להסכים
yaskimu	*taskimu*	*naskim*	*taskim*	*yaskim*	*taskimi*	*taskim*	*askim*	*lehaskim*
יתאימו	תתאימו	נתאים	תתאים	יתאים	תתאימי	תתאים	אתאים	להתאים
yat'imu	*tat'imu*	*nat'im*	*tat'im*	*yat'im*	*tat'imi*	*tat'im*	*at'im*	*lehat'im*
יתחילו	תתחילו	נתחיל	תתחיל	יתחיל	תתחילי	תתחיל	אתחיל	להתחיל
yatħilu	*tatħilu*	*natħil*	*tatħil*	*yatħil*	*tatħili*	*tatħil*	*atħil*	*lehatħil*
יציעו	תציעו	נציע	תציע	יציע	תציעי	תציע	אציע	להציע
yatsi'u	*tatsi'u*	*natsi'a*	*tatsi'a*	*yatsi'a*	*tatsi'i*	*tatsi'a*	*atsi'a*	*lehatsi'a*
יצליחו	תצליחו	נצליח	תצליח	יצליח	תצליחי	תצליח	אצליח	להצליח
yatsliħu	*tatsliħu*	*natsliaħ*	*tatsliaħ*	*yatsliaħ*	*tatsliħi*	*tatsliaħ*	*atsliaħ*	*lehatsliaħ*
יביאו	תביאו	נביא	תביא	יביא	תביאי	תביא	אביא	להביא
yavi'u	*tavi'u*	*navi*	*tavi*	*yavi*	*tavi'i*	*tavi*	*avi*	*lehavi*
יבינו	תבינו	נבין	תבין	יבין	תבינה	תבין	אבין	להבין
yavinu	*tavinu*	*navin*	*tavin*	*yavin*	*tavini*	*tavin*	*avin*	*lehavin*

הם / הן	(אתן) / (אתם)	(אנחנו)	היא	הוא	(את)	(אתה)	(אני)	Inf.
יבריאו	תבריאו	נבריא	תבריא	יבריא	תבריאי	תבריא	אבריא	להבריא
yavri'u	*tavri'u*	*navri*	*tavri*	*yavri*	*tavri'i*	*tavri*	*avri*	*lehavri*
יבטיחו	תבטיחו	נבטיח	תבטיח	יבטיח	תבטיחי	תבטיח	אבטיח	להבטיח
yavti'ħu	*tavti'ħu*	*navti'aħ*	*tavti'aħ*	*yavti'aħ*	*tavti'ħi*	*tavti'aħ*	*avti'aħ*	*lehavti'aħ*
יזמינו	תזמינו	נזמין	תזמין	יזמין	תזמיני	תזמין	אזמין	להזמין
yazminu	*tazminu*	*nazmin*	*tazmin*	*yazmin*	*tazmini*	*tazmin*	*azmin*	*lehazmin*
ייכנסו	תיכנסו	ניכנס	תיכנס	ייכנס	תיכנסי	תיכנס	אכנס	להיכנס
yikansu	*tikansu*	*nikanes*	*tikanes*	*yikanes*	*tikansi*	*tikanes*	*ekanes*	*lehikanes*
ייפגשו	תיפגשו	ניפגש	תיפגש	ייפגש	תיפגשי	תיפגש	אפגש	להיפגש
yipagshu	*tipagshu*	*nipagesh*	*tipagesh*	*yipagesh*	*tipagshi*	*tipagesh*	*epagesh*	*lehipagesh*
יישארו	תישארו	נישאר	תישאר	יישאר	תישארי	תישאר	אשאר	להישאר
yisha'eru	*tisha'eru*	*nisha'er*	*tisha'er*	*yisha'er*	*tisha'ri*	*tisha'er*	*esha'er*	*lehisha'er*
ישתתפו	תשתתפו	נשתתף	תשתתף	ישתתף	תשתתפי	תשתתף	אשתתף	להשתתף
yishtatfu	*tishtatfu*	*nishtatef*	*tishtatef*	*yishtatef*	*tishtatfi*	*tishtatef*	*eshtatef*	*lehishtatef*
יתגעגעו	תתגעגעו	נתגעגע	תתגעגע	יתגעגע	תתגעגעי	תתגעגע	אתגעגע	להתגעגע
yitga'gi'u	*titga'gi'u*	*nitga'age'a*	*titga'age'a*	*yitga'age'a*	*titga'gi'i*	*titga'age'a*	*etga'age'a*	*lehitga'age'a*
יתחתנו	תתחתנו	נתחתן	תתחתן	יתחתן	תתחתני	תתחתן	אתחתן	להתחתן
yitħatnu	*titħatnu*	*nitħaten*	*titħaten*	*yitħaten*	*titħatni*	*titħaten*	*etħaten*	*lehitħaten*
יתעוררו	תתעוררו	נתעורר	תתעורר	יתעורר	תתעוררי	תתעורר	אתעורר	להתעורר
yit'orru	*tit'orru*	*nit'orer*	*tit'orer*	*yit'orer*	*tit'orri*	*tit'orer*	*et'orer*	*lehitorer*
יתפללו	תתפללו	נתפלל	תתפלל	יתפלל	תתפללי	תתפלל	אתפלל	להתפלל
yitpallu	*titpallu*	*nitpalel*	*titpalel*	*yitpalel*	*titpalli*	*titpalel*	*etpalel*	*lehitpalel*

הם / הן	(אתן) / (אתם)	(אנחנו)	היא	הוא	(את)	(אתה)	(אני)	Inf.
יתרגלו	תתרגלו	נתרגל	תתרגל	יתרגל	תתרגלי	תתרגל	אתרגל	להתרגל
yitraglu	*titraglu*	*nitragel*	*titragel*	*yitragel*	*titragli*	*titragel*	*etragel*	*lehitragel*
יתרגשו	תתרגשו	נתרגש	תתרגש	יתרגש	תתרגשי	תתרגש	אתרגש	להתרגש
yitragshu	*titragshu*	*nitragesh*	*titragesh*	*yitragesh*	*titragshi*	*titragesh*	*etragesh*	*lehitragesh*
יתרחצו	תתרחצו	נתרחץ	תתרחץ	יתרחץ	תתרחצי	תתרחץ	אתרחץ	להתרחץ
yitraħtsu	*titraħtsu*	*nitraħets*	*titraħets*	*yitraħets*	*titraħtsi*	*titraħets*	*etraħets*	*lehitraħets*
יתקשרו	תתקשרו	נתקשר	תתקשר	יתקשר	תתקשרי	תתקשר	אתקשר	להתקשר
yitkashru	*titkashru*	*nitkasher*	*titkasher*	*yitkasher*	*titkashri*	*titkashers*	*etkashers*	*lehitkasher*
יצטערו	תצטערו	נצטער	תצטער	יצטער	תצטערי	תצטער	אצטער	להצטער
yitsta'ru	*titsta'ru*	*nitsta'er*	*titsta'er*	*yitsta'er*	*titsta'ri*	*titsta'er*	*etsta'er*	*lehitsta'er*
יוציאו	תוציאו	נוציא	תוציא	יוציא	תוציאי	תוציא	אוציא	להוציא
yotsi'u	*totsi'u*	*notsi*	*totsi*	*yotsi*	*totsi'i*	*totsi*	*otsi*	*lehotsi*
יקבלו	תקבלו	נקבל	תקבל	יקבל	תקבלי	תקבל	אקבל	לקבל
yikablu	*tikablu*	*nikabel*	*tikabel*	*yikabel*	*tikabli*	*tikabel*	*ekabel*	*lekabel*
ינגנו	תנגנו	ננגן	תנגן	ינגן	תנגני	תנגן	אנגן	לנגן
yinagnu	*tinagnu*	*ninagen*	*tinagen*	*yinagen*	*tinagni*	*tinagen*	*enagen*	*lenagen*
ינקו	תנקו	ננקה	תנקה	ינקה	תנקי	תנקה	אנקה	לנקות
yinaku	*tinaku*	*ninake*	*tinake*	*yinake*	*tinaki*	*tinake*	*anake*	*lenakot*
ירפאו	תרפאו	נרפא	תרפא	ירפא	תרפאי	תרפא	ארפא	לרפא
yirapu	*tirapu*	*nirape*	*tirape*	*yirape*	*tirapi*	*tirape*	*erape*	*lerape*
יסדרו	תסדרו	נסדר	תסדר	יסדר	תסדרי	תסדר	אסדר	לסדר
yisadru	*tisadru*	*nisader*	*tisader*	*yisader*	*tisadri*	*tisader*	*esader*	*lesader*

הם / הן	(אתן) / (אתם)	(אנחנו)	היא	הוא	(את)	(אתה)	(אני)	Inf.
יסיימו	תסיימו	נסיים	תסיים	יסיים	תסיימי	תסיים	אסיים	לסיים
yisaymu	tisaymu	nisayem	tisayem	yisayem	tisaymi	tisayem	esayem	lesayem
ישלמו	תשלמו	נשלם	תשלם	ישלם	תשלמי	תשלם	אשלם	לשלם
yishalmu	tishalmu	nishalem	tishalem	yishalem	tishalmi	tishalem	eshalem	leshalem
יטיילו	תטיילו	נטייל	תטייל	יטייל	תטיילי	תטייל	אטייל	לטייל
yitaylu	titaylu	nitayel	titayel	yitayel	titayli	titayel	etayel	letayel
יבקרו	תבקרו	נבקר	תבקר	יבקר	תבקרי	תבקר	אבקר	לבקר
yivakru	tivakru	nivaker	tivaker	yivaker	tivakri	tivaker	evaker	levaker
יבקשו	תבקשו	נבקש	תבקש	יבקש	תבקשי	תבקש	אבקש	לבקש
yivakshu	tivakshu	nivakesh	tivakesh	yivakesh	tivakshi	tivakesh	evakesh	levakesh
יבשלו	תבשלו	נבשל	תבשל	יבשל	תבשלי	תבשל	אבשל	לבשל
yivashlu	tivashlu	nivashel	tivashel	yivashel	tivashli	tivashel	evashel	levashel
יפגשו	תפגשו	נפגוש	תפגוש	יפגוש	תפגשי	תפגוש	אפגוש	לפגוש
yifigshu	tifigshu	nifgosh	tifgosh	yifgosh	tifigshi	tifgosh	efgosh	lifgosh
יפחדו	תפחדו	נפחד	תפחד	יפחד	תפחדי	תפחד	אפחד	לפחוד
yifħadu	tifħadu	nifħad	tifħad	yifħad	tifħadi	tifħad	efħad	lifħod
יכאבו	תכאבו	נכאב	תכאב	יכאב	תכאבי	תכאב	אכאב	לכאוב
yiħ'avu	tiħ'avu	niħ'av	tiħ'av	yiħ'av	tiħ'avi	tiħ'av	eħ'av	liħ'ov
יכתבו	תכתבו	נכתוב	תכתוב	יכתוב	תכתבי	תכתוב	אכתוב	לכתוב
yiħtvu	tiħtvu	niħtov	tiħtov	yiħtov	tiħtvi	tiħtov	eħtov	liħtov
יקנו	תקנו	נקנה	תקנה	יקנה	תקני	תקנה	אקנה	לקנות
yiknu	tiknu	nikne	tikne	yikne	tikni	tikne	ekne	liknot

הם / הן	(אתן) / (אתם)	(אנחנו)	היא	הוא	(את)	(אתה)	(אני)	Inf.
יקראו	תקראו	נקרא	תקרא	יקרא	תקראי	תקרא	אקרא	לקרוא
yikir'u	*tikir'u*	*nikra*	*tikra*	*yikra*	*tikir'i*	*tikra*	*ekra*	*likro'*
ילבשו	תלבשו	נלבש	תלבש	ילבש	תלבשי	תלבש	אלבש	ללבוש
yilibshu	*tilibshu*	*nilbash*	*tilbash*	*yilbash*	*tilibshi*	*tilbash*	*elbash*	*lilbosh*
ילמדו	תלמדו	נלמוד	תלמוד	ילמוד	תלמדי	תלמוד	אלמוד	ללמוד
yilimdu	*tilimdu*	*nilmod*	*tilmod*	*yilmod*	*tilimdi*	*tilmod*	*elmod*	*lilmod*
ימכרו	תמכרו	נמכור	תמכור	ימכור	תמכרי	תמכור	אמכור	למכור
yimikru	*timikru*	*nimkor*	*timkor*	*yimkor*	*timikri*	*timkor*	*emkor*	*limkor*
ימצא	תמצאו	נמצא	תמצא	ימצא	תמצאי	תמצא	אמצא	למצוא
yimitsu	*timitsu*	*nimtsa*	*timtsa*	*yimtsa*	*timitsi*	*timtsa*	*emtsa*	*limtso*
ינהגו	תנהגו	ננהג	תנהג	ינהג	תנהגי	תנהג	אנהג	לנהוג
yinhagu	*tinhagu*	*ninhag*	*tinhag*	*yinhag*	*tinhagi*	*tinhag*	*enhag*	*linhog*
ייסעו	תיסעו	ניסע	תיסע	ייסע	תיסעי	תיסע	אסע	לנסוע
yis'u	*tis'u*	*nisa*	*tisa*	*yisa*	*tis'i*	*tisa*	*esa*	*linso'a*
יראו	תראו	נראה	תראה	יראה	תראי	תראה	אראה	לראות
yir'u	*tir'u*	*nir'e*	*tir'e*	*yir'e*	*tir'i*	*tir'e*	*er'e*	*lir'ot*
ירקדו	תרקדו	נרקוד	תרקוד	ירקוד	תרקדי	תרקוד	ארקוד	לרקוד
yirikdu	*tirikdu*	*nirkod*	*tirkod*	*yirkod*	*tirikdi*	*tirkod*	*erkod*	*lirkod*
ירשמו	תרשמו	נרשום	תרשום	ירשום	תרשמי	תרשום	ארשום	לרשום
yirishmu	*tirishmu*	*nirshom*	*tirshom*	*yirshom*	*tirishmi*	*tirshom*	*ershom*	*lirshom*
ירצו	תרצו	נרצה	תרצה	ירצה	תרצי	תרצה	ארצה	לרצות
yirtsu	*tirtsu*	*nirtse*	*tirtse*	*yirtse*	*tirtsi*	*tirtse*	*ertse*	*lirtsot*

הם / הן	(אתן) / (אתם)	(אנחנו)	היא	הוא	(את)	(אתה)	(אני)	Inf.
ישאלו	תשאלו	נשאל	תשאל	ישאל	תשאלי	תשאל	אשאל	לשאול
yish'alu	tish'alu	nish'al	tish'al	yish'al	tish'ali	tish'al	esh'al	lish'ol
ישכחו	תשכחו	נשכח	תשכח	ישכח	תשכחי	תשכח	אשכח	לשכוח
yishikħu	tishikħu	nishkaħ	tishkaħ	yishkaħ	tishikħi	tishkaħ	eshkaħ	lishko'aħ
ישלחו	תשלחו	נשלח	תשלח	ישלח	תשלחי	תשלח	אשלח	לשלוח
yishilħu	tishilħu	nishlaħ	tishlaħ	yishlaħ	tishilħi	tishlaħ	eshlaħ	lishlo'aħ
ישמעו	תשמעו	נשמע	תשמע	ישמע	תשמעי	תשמע	אשמע	לשמוע
yishim'u	tishim'u	nishma	tishma	yishma	tishim'i	tishma	eshma	lishmo'a
יישנו	תישנו	נישן	תישן	יישן	תישני	תישן	אישן	לישון
yishnu	tishnu	nishen	tishen	yishen	tishni	tishen	eshen	lishon
ישחו	תשחו	נשחה	תשחה	ישחה	תשחי	תשחה	אשחה	לשחות
yisħu	tisħu	nisħe	tisħe	yisħe	tisħi	tisħe	esħe	lisħot
ישתו	תשתו	נשתה	תשתה	ישתה	תשתי	תשתה	אשתה	לשתות
yishtu	tishtu	nishte	tishte	yishte	tishti	tishte	eshte	lishtot
ישכרו	תשכרו	נשכור	תשכור	ישכור	תשכרי	תשכור	אשכור	לשכור
yisikru	tisikru	niskor	tiskor	yiskor	tisikri	tiskor	eskor	liskor
יבדקו	תבדקו	נבדוק	תבדוק	יבדוק	תבדקי	תבדוק	אבדוק	לבדוק
yivdku	tivdku	nivdok	tivdok	yivdok	tivdki	tivdok	evdok	livdok
יאמרו	תאמרו	נאמר	תאמר	יאמר	תאמרי	תאמר	אומר	לומר\ לאמור
yomru	tomru	nomar	tomar	yomar	tomri	tomar	omar	lomar

Note: The subject pronouns in the brackets do not have to be used with the verb.